FIGHTING for ~~WITH~~ YOUR FAMILY

CRAIG THOMPSON

Fighting ~~With~~ *FOR* Your Family

Spiritual Warfare and the Family

© 2025 Ordinary Christian Ministries

Craig Thompson, Author

Ginger Chestnut, Designer and Editor

All rights reserved.

No part of this publication may be reproduced, stored in a retrieval system, or transmitted in any form or by any means, electronic, mechanical, photocopying, recording or otherwise without the prior permission of the publisher or in accordance with the provisions of the Copyright, Designs and Patents Act 1988 or under the terms of any license permitting limited copying issued by the Copyright Licensing Agency.

Published by: Ordinary Christian Ministries

Cover Design by: Ginger Chestnut

Graphics and designs created in Canva.

Unless otherwise stated, Scripture passages are taken from the ESV® Study Bible (The Holy Bible, English Standard Version®), Copyright © 2008 by Crossway, a publishing ministry of Good News Publishers. Used by permission. All rights reserved.

All emphases in Scripture quotations have been added by the author.

ISBN: 978-1-965968-03-1

Dewey Decimal Classification: 248.8

Subject Headings: Religion/Christian Living/Marriage/Family/Relationships, Parenting

Fighting ~~With~~ *FOR* Your Family

Spiritual Warfare and the Family

CRAIG THOMPSON

Contents

CHAPTER ONE

Basic Training	21
The Three Fronts of Battle	*24*
The Battle with the Flesh	*25*
The Battle with the World	*29*
The Battle with Satan	*33*
Be Vigilant, but Not Paranoid	*36*

PRACTICAL APPLICATION

Give No Quarter	38
Make No Provision	*39*

CHAPTER TWO

The Battle for Leadership	42
Husbands Loving as Christ Loved His Church	*54*
Wives Loving Through Submission	*61*
The Pride Problem	*65*

PRACTICAL APPLICATION

Family Cooking and Messy Kitchens	70
Healthy Eating	*73*
Life Skills	*74*
Confidence	*76*
Service	*77*

CHAPTER THREE

The Challenge of Commitment	79
Overcoming the Obstacles to Commitment	*83*
Experiencing the Freedom of Commitment	*87*

Trust God's Word and Fight for Commitment	*91*
PRACTICAL APPLICATION	
Tablecloths	94
CHAPTER FOUR	
The Battle for Your Children	100
Don't Crowdsource Your Parenting	*107*
A Team Approach Toward Parenting	*112*
There is Strength in Numbers	*114*
PRACTICAL APPLICATION	
We Bought a Fire Pit	122
CHAPTER FIVE	
Fighting for Intimacy	133
Recognize the Need for Intimacy	*136*
Understand the Concept of Intimacy	*139*
Make a Plan for Intimacy	*143*
Deny Satan a Foothold	*147*
PRACTICAL APPLICATION	
Guarding Intimacy	148
CHAPTER SIX	
Fighting for Holiness	151
Pursue Christ Personally	*158*
Provide Space and Time for Your Spouse to Pursue Christ Devotionally	*159*
Pursue Christ Together	*160*
Regularly Communicate Commitment	*161*
Carry the Load	*162*
Set Boundaries	*167*

PRACTICAL APPLICATION

The Armor of God	170

CHAPTER SEVEN

Physical Health	175
Glorify God with Your Body	*176*
Physical Health Affects Spiritual Health	*177*
Living Sanctuary	*179*
Self-Control and Self-Discipline	*181*
Increased Capacity to Serve God	*184*
Increased Capacity to Fight for Your Family	*185*
How Do You Get There?	*187*

PRACTICAL APPLICATION

When You Have Health Issues Beyond Your Control

191

CONCLUSION

THE BATTLE OF OUR LIVES	194
Spiritual Warfare Is Real	*194*
Marriage Is Hard	*195*
Commitment Is Sexy	*197*
Raising Kids Is a Battle All Its Own	*197*
Sex Is Spiritual Warfare	*199*
Holiness Is Wholeness	*199*
A Healthy Lifestyle Is a Spiritual Discipline	*200*
Failure Is Not an Option	*200*

APPENDIX

SPIRITUAL WARFARE AND ORPHAN CARE	202
Books & Resources	209

Acknowledgments

I dedicate this book to my parents who showed me day in and day out what a healthy marriage looks like. I am well past forty years old, and I still have never heard either of my parents raise their voice in anger at each other or call one another a nasty name in a fit of rage.

Of course, this book would never exist if it were entirely up to me. Ginger Chestnut is the greatest editor and designer I could hope for. She manages me well and handles all the design and layout for publishing through Ordinary Christian Ministries. The members and staff of Malvern Hill continue to support me and to be an incredible faith community for me and my family. I am also grateful for the dozens of couples through the years who have allowed me to be part of their journey from broken relationships to wholeness and restoration. I have learned as I have walked with them through hurts and pains.

Finally, as always, I am thankful to my family. When I am at my best, I fight alongside them to be the people God has called us to be. At my worst, they have seen me fight with them, but through it all, God is kind and gracious to help us be a pretty enjoyable party of six who enjoy being together. Angela, thank you for 20 years. Wyatt, Aubrey, Brooklyn, and Sloan, thank you for being my kids. I love you all!

Fighting ~~With~~ *FOR* Your Family

Spiritual Warfare and the Family

CRAIG THOMPSON

Introduction

There we were. Staring into the future and waiting for wise advice on marriage. Angela and I had scheduled our week around this important meeting where we were going to hear sage wisdom on marriage. We had been invited into the home of a pastor and his wife for pre-marital counseling. They were warm and welcoming. We were anxious to hear all the advice they could give us on marriage. Instead, we heard, "You're going to be a pastor, so you've got all of this figured out anyway." Those were the words from the pastor who was supposed to be offering guidance to me and my future wife on how to have a "successful" marriage. There you have it—Angela and I were informed that getting married really isn't that big of a deal, and if you are going to be a pastor, you already have everything figured out.

Beyond the call of God into ministry, there were other factors that caused people to assume Angela and I had it all figured out. We came from families that most people would consider healthy. Our dads loved our moms. Our moms loved our dads. Our grandparents loved each other. We came from good stock, and we had the church "drug" problem—"drug" there every time the doors were opened. We grew up in the church and were active in it. I suppose people assumed that, given our history, we knew all we needed to know to have a healthy marriage.

With all that knowledge under our belts, how hard could it be to get married and raise a family? After all, the Bible is full of examples and instructions—from the first man and woman to plenty of scriptural advice found in Proverbs and Ephesians. We were assured that having a healthy family would come naturally to us because I was a pastor and she was going to be the wife of a pastor. Piece of cake. Right?

Truthfully, we had no clue what we were doing.

Despite our upbringing filled with intact families, we knew that families often looked very little like God intended. Divorce happens, abuse happens, neglect happens, and children are not always raised to know the Lord. Even families that are intact and look healthy from the outside are often filled with strife behind closed doors. We've learned firsthand that marriage is challenging, and when a kid—or four—comes along, it gets even more difficult. Now, twenty years into our life together, Angela and I have found raising a family to be the most rewarding and challenging experience of our married life.

I write this book because I know that marriage is difficult, and just as we did not have it all figured out, I'm sure you don't either. I write because marriage is wonderful, and I want you to experience the same joys and celebrations that we have enjoyed as a married couple. I write because we have made a few mistakes along the way that you can learn from, and because we have enjoyed a few victories that I want to share with you.

Our family began with two people born in 1981 and has grown to include four children and two German Shorthaired Pointers. Our family began with our wedding and has grown with births and adoptions. We have buried loved ones, bought and sold houses, thrived through a pandemic, and survived a few disagreements. Along the way, we have learned that Satan wants to destroy marriages, and he desires to convince us that the real enemy sleeps with us in the same home. Even more, we have learned that we are not enemies, but allies on this journey, striving together to build a healthy, happy home that honors Christ and has a positive impact on our family and the world beyond our household.

> Along the way, we have learned that Satan wants to destroy marriages, and he desires to convince us that the real enemy sleeps with us in the same home.

We had our first child (Wyatt) less than two years after we were married, and Aubrey came along 19 months later. We knew that our family was not complete, so after prayer, we opened our home up to foster children with the hope of adopting another child one day. Supposedly, the most difficult parenting transition is going from two kids to three. Comedian Jim Gaffigan joked, "Do you want to know what having a fourth kid is like? Imagine you are drowning, and someone hands you a baby." Ten years and two kids into our marriage, we didn't go from two to three; we went from two to four kids at one time.

Our youngest two children came to us through foster care and adoption at the same time. Suddenly, there we were, a party of six. We felt at times as though we were drowning with the arrival of two toddlers.

The arrival of Sloan and Brooklyn into our home brought about a time of intense struggle. Our two older kids, Wyatt and Aubrey, fared better than Angela and I did, but there were still significant challenges. Our existing family culture clashed with the struggles of transition, pain, rejection, and hurt from our foster/adopted children's pasts. The deliberate family routines that we had carefully built went out the window, and life became very hard, very quickly. In his book, *Ordinary*, Tony Merida recounts his family's adoption story this way:

> It's challenging. Doing orphan care isn't easy. My wife says she never struggled with cussing until she became a mother. Some days I think we will have been successful parents if we keep them out of prison; other days, I think we will

have been successful if I stay out of prison.[1]

Angela and I lived that statement. When I shared Merida's story with her, Angela said, "I know, right?" Her cute, "the struggle is real" tone was overshadowed only by a sigh of relief as she shared, "I'm glad I'm not the only one. I have really struggled with that over the past few months."

I want to share these details of our adoption story, not only because they are part of what makes our family what it is, but also because we have heard the exact same thing from others who are struggling not only with foster care and adoption but also with all other sorts of marriage and parenting struggles as well. One of Satan's most effective strategies is to convince us that we are the only ones going through these hard times. Our adoption story is not really unique-it is strikingly similar to the experience of almost every adoptive family we know.

Prior to adoption, we experienced other struggles in our marriage. We struggled with the deaths of family members. We had been hurt by friends and church members. We had grieved and endured alongside our

---
[1] Merida, Tony. *Ordinary*. Nashville: B&H Publishing Groups, 2015. p. 62.

church family. Even with our two older children, there had been struggles. For instance, our oldest daughter experienced two surgery-requiring bone breaks within two years. Though we had faced a few trials, nothing compared to, or had prepared us for, the struggle of adjusting to life with two new family members who did not know us—or trust us to love them unconditionally.

On more than one occasion, we battled with hopelessness. We wrestled with the real feeling and question of whether we could actually do this momentous task. I know we aren't the only parents who have wrestled with hopelessness. Most of you who are reading this book have asked yourself similar questions at some point in your marriage or parenting journey.

I'll never forget my first real struggle with hopelessness. It was Christmas Eve, and all I wanted to do was have an enjoyable family holiday celebrating Christ's birth. Christmas is my favorite time of year, but I was far from joyful. Sloan and Brooklyn had been with us less than a month, and Christmas was proving to be more nightmare than fantasy. It was so hot in South Carolina that year that our kids played in mud puddles while wearing shorts on Christmas Eve. And to top it off, our air conditioner was broken. Christmas in South Carolina is not supposed to be sultry, but, in many ways, the unseasonable Christmas weather and broken air conditioner were appropriate in light of the other struggles of that season. These physical realities gave concrete expression to the frustration, fear, and trials we experienced every day during that period of adjustment.

The day had been difficult, but I was looking forward to preaching our Christmas Eve service and coming home to our Christmas Eve dinner. I preached, and then, in the heat of all of my frustration, I yelled at my kids the entire way home from worship. The... whole... way.

#pastorfail.

I was miserable. I was angry. I was sad. I was frustrated. I was scared that life might not ever be normal again. What if every Christmas for the rest of my life was going to be this miserable?

I was mad, but I didn't know who to be mad at. I was just tired, hot, and mad, but the kids didn't deserve my anger. After blowing my stack, we made it home, and I sent them to their rooms, and then I sobbed at our kitchen sink. My sweet wife could only stand by my side and rub my back.

I felt like Alexander, the lead character of one of my favorite children's books—I was having a terrible, horrible, no good, very bad day.[2]

Suddenly, we realized we needed gift cards on Christmas Eve. I rushed to the drugstore, and with eyes that were still swollen from crying, I made my purchase. I avoided other Christmas Eve shoppers

---

[2] Viorst, Judith. *Alexander and the Terrible, Horrible, No Good, Very Bad Day*. Scholastic, 1972.

carefully. And then, I climbed into my truck to return home, where I seemed to be actively ruining Christmas Eve for my whole family.

Merry. Christmas.

I share that story only so that you will know we understand a few things about struggles in our home. In the midst of that really difficult time, it was sometimes easy to point blame at all of the people who were making my life miserable. But the truth is, the blame for all that misery belonged first and foremost to Satan and sin. And no... not the sin you might think. Most of my misery and struggle in those moments was not the result of the sin that left Sloan and Brooklyn orphans—my misery was the result of *my* sin.

> Most of my misery and struggle was not the result of the sin of others. My misery was the result of *my* sin.

It turns out I was selfish, impatient, short-tempered, and far too reliant on my own strength and abilities, rather than upon the Spirit of God. It turns out that I was a very imperfect man with a slightly less imperfect wife trying to raise imperfect children in the fear and admonition of the Lord. We were in a battle, and in that moment, we were losing.

If you are married or are contemplating marriage, whether you have children or not, you, too, will battle with Satan and sin. You will struggle as a result of the sin of others for sure, but *your* sin is what needs to be dealt with first. Just like me, as your marriage progresses and your family grows, you will discover that there is sin in your heart that needs to be repented of. Your family will probably prove to be your most fertile ground for personal sanctification.

The purpose of this book is to equip you to engage in spiritual warfare for your family—to learn to fight for your family instead of against them. As I wrote above, it can be difficult at times to know with whom we should be angry—we don't even know who to blame. Spiritual warfare is a reality, and just as it is real in your personal life and in your local church, spiritual warfare is real in your family. I want to teach you how to fight. We will begin by considering what spiritual warfare is in a general sense and look at how we can put on the whole armor of God. After the first chapter, the remainder of the book will focus on the specifics of engaging in spiritual warfare for, and alongside, your family.

Let's get started!

CHAPTER ONE

Basic Training

When two humans have lived together for many years, it usually happens that each has tones of voice and expressions of face which are almost unendurably irritating to the other. Work on that. Bring fully into the consciousness of your patient that particular lift of his mother's eyebrows which he learned to dislike in the nursery, and let him think how much he dislikes it. Let him assume that she knows how annoying it is and does it to annoy - if you know your job, he will not notice the immense improbability of the assumption. And, of course, never let him suspect that he has tones and looks which similarly annoy her. As he cannot see or hear himself, this is easily managed.

-C.S. Lewis, The Screwtape Letters

The quote above is C. S. Lewis's attempt to verbalize how he believes Satan may tempt families to turn on one another. Lewis's fictional account—an imaginative tale of how Satan and his demons might attack and corrupt a human "patient"— helps the reader understand how demonic forces might work against families and marriages. In marriage counseling, I remind couples that Satan is the enemy, your spouse is not. Unfortunately, Satan does his best work when he convinces you that he is not involved in your discord at all. If Satan showed up in your marriage announcing, "I've come to destroy your relationship," everyone would recognize his divisive nature and run the other way. Instead, he comes disguised as an angel of light. Instead of promising division, Satan and his demons come into your marriage promising happiness or fulfillment—often fulfillment in the form of something or someone other than the wife or

> Satan is the enemy, your spouse is not. Satan wants you to believe that your spouse is the obstacle to your happiness.

husband of your youth.[1] Once you have bought into his promise, he then begins to suggest that your spouse is an obstacle to your happiness. Christians must learn to identify satanic influence in our lives and in our marriages and to address it biblically. The goal of this book is to help you do just that.

In his book, *God, Marriage, and Family*, Andreas Kostenberger argues that discord and divorce are directly related to demonic engagement:

> Arguably, divorce rates are skyrocketing, not primarily because of the lack of good intentions, the unavailability of resources and instruction on how to conduct a strong biblical marriage, or even the lack of love, but because many unbelievers and believers alike inadequately recognize that spiritual warfare is a certain reality that calls for a concerted, deliberately planned response.[2]

In all discord in our homes, the ultimate enemy is not your spouse, your children, their biological parents, their former foster parents, DSS, the school district, or anyone else. Satan is the ultimate enemy. He has the destruction of God's people as one of his ultimate goals. The family, the primary unit of God's

---
[1] Malachi 2:14
[2] Kostenberge,Andreas Jr. and Jones, David W. *God, Marriage, and Family.* Crossway, 2004). p.167.

> The family, the primary unit of God's good design for his children, and Satan's number one target. Your home is a battleground for spiritual warfare.

good design for his children, is Satan's number one target.

Your home is a battleground for spiritual warfare. For many Christians, spiritual warfare is more of a fairy tale drawn in comic book style on large boards, the scenes depicted in the local "hell house," or the stuff that missionaries to the Congo experience. But spiritual warfare is a reality in your family and mine. The purpose of this book is to equip you to engage in spiritual warfare for and with your family. To do so, we must first understand a little bit about spiritual warfare.

The Three Fronts of Battle

Spiritual warfare is fought on three primary fronts: the battle with the flesh, the battle with the world, and the battle with Satan and demons. *The flesh* is the very real struggle that you have with yourself and your own desires. *The world* is the environment in which we live that works to direct our attention away from the things of Christ. *Satan* is a personal and intelligent spirit being who is opposed to Christ and his children. *Demons* are fallen angels and emissaries of Satan who work to do Satan's bidding in this world.

The Battle with the Flesh

The struggle against the pull of the world and the battle with Satan and demons piques our interest, but your own flesh is the first front in spiritual warfare. Healthy families are led by husbands and wives who focus first on the battle with their own flesh. It is easy to blame problems on outside issues; however, the greatest enemy you will face in the battle for your family is usually the enemy that stares back in the mirror every morning.

If you need some help understanding this battle with the flesh, just consider what happens when you oversleep on a school morning. You know that you messed up, but do you take full responsibility or allow your frustrations to spill over into your relationships? It is so tempting to wake up thirty minutes late and immediately ask, "Honey, why didn't *you* set *your* alarm?" or to growl at your kids, "What is taking *you* so long?" See the problem here? *You* are the first front that you must battle in order to be successful in spiritual warfare. I know this is true because the greatest enemy I face in my house is me.

> The greatest enemy you will face in the battle for your family is usually the enemy that stares back in the mirror every morning.

Most beliefs about spiritual warfare are geared

toward defeating Satan and other spirit beings. It is important to know how to oppose the demonic, but you should also know that Satan is content to leave you alone if he doesn't have to engage you personally. His engagement is not necessary if you are willing to surrender to your fleshly desires. The primary battle is against flesh and blood. Consider Paul's words in Ephesians 2:1-3:

> *And you were dead in the trespasses and sins in which you once walked, following the course of this world, following the prince of the power of the air, the spirit that is now at work in the sons of disobedience— among whom we all once lived in the passions of our flesh, carrying out the desires of the body and the mind, and were by nature children of wrath, like the rest of mankind.*

The Christian's most consistent enemy is his own flesh, but in Christ, we have the power to resist our worldly desires.[3]

Later in Ephesians 6:12, Paul's words point to the power of spiritual authorities and cosmic powers,

> *For we do not wrestle against flesh and blood, but against the rulers, against the authorities, against the cosmic powers over this present dark-*

---
[3] 1 Corinthians 10:13

ness, against the spiritual forces of evil in the heavenly places.

However, there is no contradiction in terms between Ephesians 2 and Ephesians 6. In the latter passage, Paul warns that the battle is not with flesh and blood. The difference is that Paul is writing in Ephesians 2 about the battle with one's own flesh. In Ephesians 6, the battle being described is not internal conflict against the sinful passions of the flesh, but an external conflict with the powers of darkness. The battle against the flesh is real but often overlooked by people who feel an unhealthy sense of ownership over their own bodies.

Returning to *The Screwtape Letters*, C. S. Lewis characterizes it this way,

> Much of the modern resistance to chastity comes from men's belief that they 'own' their bodies—those vast and perilous estates, pulsating with the energy that made the worlds, in which they find themselves without their consent and from which they are ejected at the pleasure of Another![4]

There is no spiritual neutrality. Everyone serves someone— God or Satan.[5] Indulging in the flesh will lead you to accomplish the will of the devil without

---
[4] Lewis, C. S. *The Screwtape Letters*. Harper Collins, 1942. p. 113.
[5] In John 8:44, Jesus warns the Pharisees that "If God were your father, you would love me," but because they do not love him they belong to "your father, the devil."

his involvement. You will do the devil's dirty work all by yourself. Satan often wins because we are easy prey, gratifying the desires of the flesh to our own detriment and his victory.[6]

> There is no spiritual neutrality. Everyone serves someone— God or Satan.

The battle with the flesh is shown clearly in other passages of scripture as well. The book of James contrasts fleshly desires with godly accomplishments,

> *Know this, my beloved brothers: let every person be quick to hear, slow to speak, slow to anger; for the anger of man does not produce the righteousness of God. Therefore, put away all filthiness and rampant wickedness and receive with meekness the implanted word, which is able to save your souls.*[7]

You will never achieve godly goals in the power of your flesh. If you choose to gratify the anger you feel every time your spouse frustrates you, there is little chance of you living in spiritual victory. Instead, you will see Satan claiming territory in your family without having to fire a single shot.

In the battle for your family, you must first confront your own flesh and bring it under control. As you fight

---

[6] Lawless, Chuck. *Discipled Warriors*, p. 18.
[7] James 1:19-21

with your flesh and bring it under the control of the Holy Spirit, you will be better prepared for battle on the other two fronts. In Romans 12:1, Paul urges the Roman believers to "present your bodies as a living sacrifice, holy and acceptable to God, which is your spiritual worship." Even as Paul begs the question of how to offer your body as a spiritual sacrifice, he offers God's answer:

> *Do not be conformed to this world, but be transformed by the renewal of your mind, that by testing you may discern what is the will of God, what is good and acceptable and perfect.*[8]

The Battle with the World

The battle against the flesh overlaps with the battle against the world. As you work to bring your sinful nature under control through the Word of God and the Holy Spirit, God is using that Word to transform your mind. Time spent in God's word changes us and allows us to present our flesh to God. It also changes our worldview, enabling us to no longer be conformed to the world, but to be different from the world. So, what is "the world?"

The "world" embodies all the cultural influences experienced by the believer. The battle with the world

---
[8] Romans 12:2

> The "world" embodies all the cultural influences experienced by the believer.

and its prevailing culture is not always as personal as the battle of the flesh. The battle with the world could be against the naturalistic/evolutionary theories taught in your kids' biology class, or transgender bathroom policies, but it is more frequently against your entertainment options and leisure decisions. The greatest worldview struggles will come through movies, books, and peers, not through freshman biology.

There are challenges in public education for sure, but do not be fooled into believing that worldview challenges only come in the classroom. Even all the way back in the late 1900s (as the kids in my church say), the Smashing Pumpkins screamed through the speakers of my 1983 Ford Ranger, "and I still believe that I cannot be saved." My Christian worldview was being attacked.

The struggle with the world is not always isolated from struggles with the devil. There are three ways in which the prince of the air works through the world to fight against the Word and will of God. First, "the enemy blinds unbelievers to the Gospel[9]." [10] The world does not see its need for the gospel because Satan has blinded people to their need for Christ. Second,

---

[9] Lawless, Chuck. *Discipled Warriors*, p.85.
[10] 2 Corinthians 4:4

Satan has filled the world with idols to be trusted and worshipped, and people tend to become what they worship.[11] Finally, idols must be obeyed. The idols of the world will ultimately form people into their image rather than into the image of Christ.

War with the world, as described in the New Testament, can also be conceived of as a war against idolatry and false gods. John even closes his first epistle with these words, "little children, keep yourselves from idols".[12] The world beckons us to bow down before all sorts of idols that promise enjoyment, fulfillment, or even family time. In many families, recreation has become an all-encompassing passion that resembles worshiping Baal more than playing ball.[13] Idolatry is a very real threat for 21st-century families, but the temptation is so subtle that you could bow down to the world's idols before you even realize your priorities have changed. You may not even realize the control your idols have until you attempt to walk away. The financial and social commitments create an expected and assumed obedience.

Peter knew this. He wrote,

> *But even if you should suffer for righteousness' sake, you will be blessed. Have no fear of them,*

---

[11] Beale, G. K. *We Become What We Worship.* IVP Academic, 2008; see also Keller, Timothy. *Counterfeit Gods.* Dutton, 2009.
[12] 1 John 5:21
[13] Eliff, Jim. "When Ball Becomes Baal," http://ftc.co/resource-library/1/2000. accessed August 1, 2016.

> *nor be troubled, but in your hearts regard Christ the Lord as holy, always being prepared to make a defense to anyone who asks you for a reason for the hope that is in you.*[14]

Peter learned the hard way. When he was asked about Jesus, he denied knowing him. Rather than risk suffering because of his relationship with Jesus, he bowed before the idol of his own safety and security.

Expect to suffer if you refuse to bow down to the idols of the world. "The Bible uses three metaphors to describe how people relate to the idols of their hearts. They love idols, trust idols, and obey idols."[15] Those who choose to love, trust, and obey God instead of the world's idols cannot expect to be celebrated by idol worshipers around them.

When you choose to be different from others by seeking God's priorities first, you will suffer, and your children might suffer a bit as well. When you choose to love, trust, and obey God rather than idols, your children may not participate in the same activities as their friends. When you commit to regular worship and church fellowship, your children will have to miss some practices, rehearsals, or even games. You may make different choices in entertainment. And you will almost certainly not have the same access to disposable income when you make kingdom-giving a priority. Parents who

---

[14] 1 Peter 3:14-15
[15] Keller, Timothy. *Counterfeit Gods*, xxi.

commit to tithing and giving to missions may not be able to afford lavish vacations every year, new cars for their teenagers, or a nice boat. But kingdom priorities must replace worldly commitments. You have to make the decision in this battle against the world. Will you store up treasures on earth or in heaven?[16]

The Battle with Satan

Satan fights back when you go to war with your flesh and resist the temptation from the world. As we saw earlier, Paul spoke of this aspect of spiritual warfare in Ephesians 6:12 as a confrontation with "the rulers, against the authorities, against the cosmic powers over this present darkness, against the spiritual forces of evil in the heavenly places." The most consistent areas of spiritual warfare in the family are with the flesh and with the world, but the battle against the evil one is a major aspect of spiritual warfare that should not be ignored. Christians must avoid the error of ignoring the existence of Satan and the reality of the spirit world in spiritual battle. Charles Spurgeon warned, "There is no believer in Christ, no follower of that which is true and lovely and of good repute,

> Satan fights back when you go to war with your flesh and resist the temptation from the world.

---
[16] Matthew 6:20

who will not find himself, in some season or other, attacked by this foul fiend and the legions enlisted in his service."[17]

Peter was concerned enough about the battle against demonic forces that he warned his readers,

> *Humble yourselves, therefore, under the mighty hand of God so that at the proper time he may exalt you, casting all your anxieties on him, because he cares for you. Be sober-minded; be watchful. Your adversary the devil prowls around like a roaring lion, seeking someone to devour. Resist him, firm in your faith, knowing that the same kinds of suffering are being experienced by your brotherhood throughout the world.* [18]

Peter emphasizes that the attack is coming, and that it is being experienced by the "brotherhood throughout the world." Spiritual attack is a common experience among believers, and one for which you must prepare. Satan will attack you and your family personally.

However, Satan's attacks are not always directly aimed at your family alone. Sometimes they are indirect ambushes. In 2 Peter 2, Peter warns against false teachers who do the devil's work. Confrontations with Satan often involve false prophets—people who have been influenced by the ways of the evil one and who seek

---
[17] Spurgeon, Charles. *Spiritual Warfare in the Believer's Life*. Lynwood, WA: Emerald, 1993. p. 100.
[18] 1 Peter 5:6-9

to bring others under his sway. False prophets are compared to the angels who were not spared by God when they sinned.[19] False prophets are dangerous weapons in Satan's arsenal as he attacks God's church. Sinclair Ferguson warns, "the most sinister thoughts that Satan suggests are not enticements to sin but suspicions about God Himself. He always plots to cause us to 'exchange the truth of God for a lie.'"[20] In Genesis 3, when Satan tempted Eve in the garden, his temptation was for her to exchange the truth of God's word for a lie. Just as Satan worked through the serpent, he can work through false teachers. When Satan can work through a teacher, he can infect an entire church.

If the danger of spiritual attack from false teachers is so great within a church, then it is also of grave concern for families. Husbands and wives, you must commit to a healthy church where the Word of God is faithfully preached. Husbands are responsible for protecting their families from false teachers and false teaching. The greatest weapon against false teaching

> The greatest weapon against false teaching is a healthy understanding of God's word developed through regular time spent reading God's word and collective discipleship within the context of a local church.

---
[19] 2 Peter 2:4
[20] Ferguson, Sinclair. *By Grace Alone*. Orlando: Reformation Trust, 2010. p. 84.

is a healthy understanding of God's word developed through regular time spent reading God's word and collective discipleship within the context of a local church. A robust personal knowledge of the Bible helps God's people to identify the wolves who invade the church and harm families.

Be Vigilant, but Not Paranoid

Where does this leave us? Be vigilant, but not paranoid, in spiritual warfare. One night during family devotions, my oldest son, who was four at the time, announced that there were three Gods. Usually, parents would chalk this up to youth, but because one of his teachers was a Mormon, I flew into heresy control (Because the Mormon religion claims there are multiple gods). My wife laid her hand on my leg and asked, "Wyatt, what do you mean?" He confidently informed us that there was the Father, the Son, and the Holy Spirit. In his four-year-old way, Wyatt was declaring his belief in the Trinity, not in the polytheistic world of Mormonism.

Crisis averted.

I saw the devil where childish ignorance and innocence loomed. In that moment, the most important spiritual battle to be fought was against ignorance, not against an attack from Satan. Parents, do not allow those instances to lull you into spiritual slumber. Always be prepared, but remember that preparation does not require paranoia. Families should be vigilant, but not paranoid. 1 Peter 5:8 warns the devil is a roaring lion looking for people to devour, but he is not around every corner. Parents, it is your responsibility to do everything you can to keep the lion of 1 Peter (the devil) away from your lambs, but you must work just as diligently to make sure that you do not become a devouring lion in your own home.

PRACTICAL APPLICATION

Give No Quarter

Spiritual warfare is a reality of life, whether you choose to acknowledge it or not. Often, spiritual warfare is misconstrued. We are tempted to either give the devil too much credit or to deny that real spiritual warfare exists at all. Giving the devil too much credit usually occurs in one of two ways: we either attribute every struggle in our lives to Satan's involvement, or we forget that, as believers, we are not fighting for victory, but from a place of victory. Colossians 2:14-15 makes this truth very clear: "This he set aside, nailing it to the cross. He disarmed the rulers and authorities and put them to open shame, by triumphing over them in him." We do not pray for victory over Satan; we are called to live into the victory that Christ has already won.

> We do not pray for victory over Satan; we are called to live into the victory that Christ has already won.

More often than not, however, our greatest struggle for purity and sanctification is not with Satan, but with ourselves. Until such time as we have found mastery over our flesh, there is little need for Satan to oppose us as believers in Christ. Paul offers great help in Romans 13. He calls on believers to walk "properly, as in the daytime" and to "put on the Lord Jesus Christ." We must regularly take up the armor of God as Paul explains further in Ephesians 6. Putting on Christ and taking up the armor should be viewed synonymously in God's word. Engaging in spiritual warfare requires believers to take up Christ, to clothe themselves in righteousness and holiness. But that's not all.

Make No Provision

Paul also urges us to "make no provision for the flesh, to gratify its desires."[1] Most of our failures are a result of our unwillingness to starve our earthly desires.

Make no provision. These words of Paul ring loudly

---
[1] Romans 13:14

in my ears as I ponder the times when I dwell on the desires of my flesh.

In military terms, to give no quarter means to show no mercy or compassion toward a defeated enemy—to take no prisoners or captives. To give no quarter requires a fight to the death, the obliteration of an enemy. International humanitarian law, since the 1907 Hague Convention, has forbidden "to declare that no quarter will be given." It is customary and binding upon parties in international conflicts to provide quarter to enemy combatants.[2]

But in your war with sin, quarter should not be given. Make no provision, give no quarter, "put to death what is earthly in you: sexual immorality, impurity, passion, evil desire, and covetousness, which is idolatry," and "put on the new self, which is being renewed in knowledge after the image of its creator."[3]

Perhaps you are not in sin, but you are lingering on the precipice of sin. Rather than starving your flesh and giving your sinful desires "no quarter," have you carved out space in your life for your sinful desires to live? Do you take a second look and gaze for just a minute as that woman passes by? Do you daydream over what you could have done with the tithe that you offered last Sunday? Do you take an extra minute to consider the rude way that you were cut off in traffic?

---

[2] https://avalon.law.yale.edu/imt/judlawre.asp
[3] Colossians 3:5-11

PRACTICAL APPLICATION

Do you peruse your social media feeds on the chance that you might sneak a peek?

Regardless of what your temptation may be, the command of Paul is that you should make no provision. You should not provide any fuel for the fire of your fleshly desires. In fact, the opposite should be true. As you put on the Lord Jesus Christ, you should be starving and smothering your sinful flesh. The righteousness of Christ and the pleasures of his word work to extinguish the flames of your sinful desires when rightly applied. Satan is a real force to be reckoned with, but he's probably not your primary foe today. More likely than not, your greatest struggle today is with the person you saw in the mirror brushing your teeth. Ponder today how it is that you may apply God's words. What changes can you make in your life right now to deny provision to your flesh and to fan into flame the gift of God that is in you?

> You should not provide any fuel for the fire of your fleshly desires.

CHAPTER TWO

The Battle for Leadership

Your desire shall be for your husband, and he shall rule over you.

Genesis 3:16b

> Marriage is agreeing to sleep in a room that is too cold beside a person who is sleeping in a room that is too hot. Conflict is inevitable.

-Source Unknown

A 1993 Reader's Digest article recounted the story of a woman who asked a room full of wives, "How many of you would like to mother your husbands?" Surprised when one woman raised her hand, the speaker asked again, "You want to mother your husband?" "Mother?!" the woman replied, "I thought you said smother."

Marriage is not always easy, and families can be messy, but the family is God's most basic and most important relational unit. Long before there was a church or a gathering for Old Testament worship in the temple, God created and ordained the family. The first family began, like all families, with a lonely man in need of the love and companionship that can only be found in a woman. Adam, probably more than any other man, could affirm the old adage that there is a good woman behind every good man. After all, he knew the loneliness of life without Eve.

God also knew of Adam's loneliness, and he knew that Adam needed a helper. So grave was the issue at hand that we see God looking at his creation and saying, "It is not good." What was not good and continues to not be good? Man being alone. This realization has caused one commentator to write that the negative response from God "over what is his otherwise 'good' creation requires his special attention. Such observation emphasizes the importance of the woman in the mind of God."[1]

The fact that God created woman as a helper is not a slander against women. Divine initiative is at center stage here.[2] God saw woman as the necessary addition for a complete and "good" creation. We can speculate that Adam was lonely, but it was God who recognized Adam's need, not Adam himself, and it was God who met that need by providing a suitable helpmate. After creating the woman, God announces that his creation is good. When human beings, the crown jewel of God's creation, are flourishing in relationship both with him and with one another, God is satisfied. God is glorified through marriages that honor each partner and honor their Creator. Understanding and applying biblical leadership and submission is imperative to winning the spiritual battle for your family.

In the very first God-created family, there was equality in creation. God created them both male and female, and they were created uniquely different from the animals. Unlike the animals, over which man was given dominion, woman was created as a suitable equal for Adam—a match that could not be found in the rest of creation. Furthermore, as Genesis 1:26-27 points out, God created both man *and* woman as his

---

[1] Matthews, Kenneth A. *The New American Commentary: Genesis 1-11:26.* Nashville, TN: Broadman and Holman Publishers, 1996. p. 212.
[2] Ibid.

image-bearers. Adam does not bear more of the image of God than does Eve, nor she more than he. It is also the case that man is not given dominion over woman; they share the responsibility of dominion over God's creation. In terms of creation, the man and the woman match up perfectly with one another as leader and helpmate ruling over God's creation. Adam and Eve complete one another.

The concept of helper is not a human creation or a result of the fall. In marriage, the roles of leader/helper are a part of God's intention. The difference in roles is not a difference in value, but in responsibility. In his defense of male leadership, Paul appeals to the creation order that the man is to lead and the wife is to follow.[3] Furthermore, it should be noted that God designates this role verbally. He doesn't create man and woman and then expect them to fill in the blanks for their roles on their own. He creates Adam and then says, "I will make him a helper." It is not good for a man to be all alone, but it is very good for him to take the primary responsibility of leadership in his marriage. The man is to take the lead in male-female relationships. As God decrees in Genesis 1:14, "Therefore a man shall leave his father and his mother and hold fast to his wife,

---

[3] 1 Timothy 2:13-14

and they shall become one flesh." God gives the initial responsibility of relational leadership to the man.[4]

Even in their different roles as leader and helper, husband and wife maintain equality in creation as image bearers of God. Bruce Ware points out that God is absolutely glorified and his image is revealed before the entire world in a godly marriage defined by masculine leadership and feminine submission.[5] Even the Trinity is illustrated to the world through marriage. As God the Holy Spirit submits to the Son and the Father and as God the Son submits to the Father and as the Father leads by giving his glory to the Son, so too the marriage relationship bears an image of the Holy Trinity through acts of servant leadership and loving submission. God calls husbands to be leaders just as he leads as Father, and he calls wives to be submissive to their husbands just as God submits through the persons of the Son and the Spirit.[6] Both man and woman equally represent God to the world as his image bearers, but they present the image of God in unique ways. Healthy

> Healthy marriages give the world a beautiful picture of the relationship that exists between Father, Son, and Spirit in the Trinity.

---

[4] I give credit for some of this line of reasoning to *Men's Fraternity*. "Men's Fraternity: Home." Men's Fraternity Classic, www.mensfraternity.com/. Accessed 19 May 2025.
[5] Ware, Bruce. *Father, Son, and Holy Spirit*. Crossway Publishers, 2005.
[6] Ibid. 145.

marriages give the world a beautiful picture of the relationship that exists between Father, Son, and Spirit in the Trinity.

Those who hold to an egalitarian worldview claim that male leadership in the home is a product of the ancient patriarchal society in which the Bible was written. The Bible presents a different, more complementary position—male leadership is a product of divine creation. The Bible also gives a clear picture of roles within the home. A proper understanding of these roles is an important component of the spiritual defense for the family.

The first sin of mankind was a sin that struck at the heart of the family. How was the sin of Eve a sin against the family? Eve's sin was born out of her desire to have authority and out of Adam's refusal to exercise leadership. The serpent was crafty, and he deceived Eve,[7] but during this time of temptation, Adam was with Eve. We can only speculate about Adam's reasoning, but we can say with confidence that Adam, and not just Eve, was guilty of wrong in that first sinful failure. Rather than standing up for, and protecting, his wife, Adam stood by as a passive spectator in her time of greatest need.

This first sin began with a role reversal that led to the struggle for leadership. Rather than leading his wife, Adam stood by and allowed his wife to lead him.

---
[7] Genesis 3:13

Adam would be lauded by feminists for his willingness to share leadership, and Eve could be celebrated for throwing off the chains of patriarchy. Adam and Eve pioneered egalitarian marriage. Regardless of how politically correct it may seem to some in our culture, their decisions did not lead to a closer walk with God or with one another. Instead, their actions created separation from God and a competition for leadership in the home, a dynamic that has plagued humanity ever since the fall.

The discussion between Adam and Eve in the marriage counselor's office could sound remarkably similar to that of couples struggling with their marriages today. I can imagine the two of them sitting in their pastor's office the week after The Fall:

Adam: This is all her fault. If she had never eaten that stupid apple, we wouldn't be in this situation.

Eve: My fault? You were standing there. Besides, if you had brought home supper, we wouldn't have needed to be out scrounging anyway.

Adam: Maybe if you were meeting more of my needs, I'd be more willing to help out around the house. All you do is nag me about helping out. I'm so tired of being nagged. Why couldn't you just cook supper?

Eve: Meet your needs? I don't even want to share the same bed with you right now. Look at what your laziness has led us to do. I'm so tired of all of your excuses.

Marital problems often begin with a struggle over leadership and degenerate into finger-pointing. The blame game is always a bad idea in marriage, but it is still a common routine in many homes. In the case of Adam and Eve, Adam even went so far as to point the finger at both Eve and God. "The woman whom *you* gave to be with me, *she* gave me the fruit of the tree, and I ate it."[8] Adam knew he had a responsibility to his wife. He acknowledged that God gave the woman to him. Adam was well aware he was responsible for her and that he was accountable to God and to his wife for his actions toward her. Adam did not act responsibly. Adam reneged on his leadership role and then played the blame game rather than accepting responsibility. Eve, on the other hand, seems to fare better at first glance. In Genesis 3:13, she says, "The serpent deceived me, and I ate." She rightly affirms the source of her temptation. She was tempted by the serpent to eat of the fruit. She also confirms that she ate the fruit. What Eve is not so quick to confess is that she ate the fruit because she desired to be like God. She wanted to be her own authority.

---
[8] Genesis 3:12, emphasis added

Ultimate authority resides in God alone. Authority in the home, however, is given to the husband: "The husband is the head of the wife even as Christ is the head of the church."[9] In the case of The Fall in the garden, the sin began with a reversal of roles. Both Adam and Eve needed to take responsibility for the areas where they had failed. Adam failed to love and lead his wife, and Eve failed to submit to his God-ordained leadership. After The Fall, husband and wife turned on one another, but there was another enemy present even before their sin.

The serpent was in the garden as the tempter, and the serpent existed as the enemy of this first family long before either man or woman saw each other as the enemy. Satan existed as the unrecognized enemy, disguising himself as a messenger of goodwill. This pattern of deception and deceit that began with the very first family continues today. The accuser of souls, the devil himself, opposes marriage because marriage is established by God. He presents himself in our world as an angel of light,[10] promising liberation from old norms or a move to greener pastures on the other side of the fence.[11] The result

> The accuser of souls, the devil himself, opposes marriage because marriage is established by God.

---

[9] Ephesians 5:23
[10] 2 Corinthians 11:14-15
[11] 2 Corinthians 11:14

of following Satan's promises is separation from those we love and from the God who loves us. Satan tempted the first family with a battle for leadership, and the battle has raged ever since.

Marriages fall prey to the lies of an enemy that lurks unseen and unopposed. Husbands and wives view each other as the enemy that must be conquered, rather than the partner given by God to overcome the enemy of souls. Men have allowed Satan to run rampant in their homes by practicing passivity in their relationships instead of taking responsibility as spiritual leaders. Women continue to desire to be their own authority, and in doing so, seek to rule over their husbands, just as God said in Genesis 3 when he told Eve that her desire would be for her husband. Eve turned God's design on its head and opened the door for temptation and the sin that follows.

Families need a radical change toward a godly way of living together in covenant with God and one another. God has appointed husbands as the spiritual leaders of their homes and has given them wives as the perfect helpmate in this spiritual battle. Instead of viewing your spouse as territory to be conquered, accept your God-given role as husband or wife and look to your spouse as a fellow soldier in a spiritual battle with eternal ramifications.

> Your spouse is a fellow soldier in a spiritual battle with eternal ramifications.

Of course, it is more than a soldier in a battle; your spouse is your friend, lover, and constant companion. Husbands and wives are to love each other selflessly. You fight for your marriage, for the glory of God, and for the love you have for one another.

The gospel of God is given not just to unbelievers to be saved, but also to believers to be constantly renewed in their relationship with God. The news that Jesus died on a cross is good news for the church, for the individual, and for the family as well. If the Spirit of God richly indwells your marriage, you can experience constant transformation—growing you more and more into the image of Christ. As you become more like him, your marriages will grow to better reflect the triune God, for all the world to see, as you submit your marriage to his design. The activity of God on the cross was a divine rescue from the captivity of sin and Satan. In the spiritual battle that is married life, husbands and wives need to live in the power of the gospel, trusting in Christ's power over sin.

Christian families need to know that the gospel has freed them from their enslavement to sin and has made them alive in Christ to live in a deep relationship with him. Because you have been saved, you now have the God-given opportunity to live out God's plan for marriage in a way that is impossible without Christ. Christian husband, you can follow Christ's example of servant leadership because you have been saved by Christ's sacrifice. Christian wife, you can follow Christ's example of submission to the Father, because you have been saved by Christ's sacrifice.

The enemy of your marriage is not your lazy husband or your unsupportive wife. The enemy of your marriage is Satan and the sin that holds your family captive when you are not living under the forgiving and releasing power of the gospel. The way of Christ is better than the way of the world. It is not necessarily easier, but it is more fulfilling, and it is honoring to a holy God. When you allow God to direct and indwell your family, he transforms your marriage. Christian marriages can work because Christians have been set free to live together through the work of Christ on the cross. The attacks from Satan will still come, but you can have the confidence that he has already been defeated on the cross.

> When you allow God to direct and indwell your family, he transforms your marriage.

Leadership in the Christian marriage begins with submission to God by both partners. The husband, as the spiritual leader and selfless lover of the home, is responsible for working to keep the family aligned with God's principles. The wife supports her husband by lovingly submitting to his leadership and honoring God with her life. This mutual relationship honors God and opposes the work of Satan in your marriage.

Husbands Loving as Christ Loved His Church

How does a husband lead his wife and family without dominating them? A husband's leadership can be demonstrated by an afternoon walk on a busy road. I once heard a pastor explain leadership by saying that he always walks next to the road so that he stands between traffic and his wife. Why? Because, as her leader and lover, he has a responsibility to protect her. Leadership in the home means that the husband is the one who should get hit by the car.

Popular ideology has led us to believe that leadership is equivalent to authoritarian rule. Christ, however, made it clear to his disciples that the leadership to which they were called was not the same as the leadership of unbelievers. Speaking to his disciples in Mark 10:42-45, Jesus said:

> *You know that those who are considered rulers of the Gentiles lord it over them, and their great ones exercise authority over them. But it shall not be so among you. But whoever would be great among you must be your servant, and whoever would be first among you must be slave of all. For even the Son of Man came not to be served but to serve, and to give his life as a ransom for many.*

Christian leadership is not intended as a show of

power. Christian leadership is rooted in sacrificial love. Jesus came not to be served, but to serve. Husbands, in your home, you shouldn't lead your wife and children by trying to dominate. You should lead them in a way that serves their best interest. Your legacy should be one of love and gentle leadership that directs your family toward Christ, not one of dominion and harsh authority. It is often best to speak of a husband's role as loving more than leading.

Understanding biblical authority and leadership is essential to developing a keen understanding of biblical roles within marriage. When the Bible says that men are to lead in the home, it is not saying that women are to submit to abuse or to the role of second-class citizens. Properly understood, God's command for male leadership in the home is not meant to demean women, but to empower the family. For example, look at Ephesians 5:22-31:

> *Wives, submit to your own husbands, as to the Lord. For the husband is the head of the wife even as Christ is the head of the church, his body, and is himself its Savior. Now as the church submits to Christ, so also wives should submit in everything to their husbands. Husbands, love your wives, as Christ loved the church and gave himself up for her, that he might sanctify her, having cleansed her by the washing of water with the word, so that he might present the church to*

himself in splendor, without spot or wrinkle or any such thing, that she might be holy and without blemish. In the same way husbands should love their wives as their own bodies. He who loves his wife loves himself. For no one ever hated his own flesh, but nourishes and cherishes it, just as Christ does the church, because we are members of his body. "Therefore a man shall leave his father and mother and hold fast to his wife, and the two shall become one flesh."

In recent years, an inordinate amount of attention has been given to the submission of the wife in verses 22-24, but the majority of this passage of Scripture is focused not on wives but on husbands. Paul emphasizes *love*, not leadership. Husbands are to love their wives as Christ loved the church—a love so great that it cost him his life. The primary command of the husband is not to lead or exercise authority, but to love. The kind of love commanded by Paul to the Ephesians is extravagant. Husbands are to love their wives at all costs, sacrificing whatever is necessary to love them completely. What does costly love look like?

> The kind of love commanded by Paul to the Ephesians is extravagant.

For too long in the Christian church, we have focused on male leadership when we should have been talking about the love of husbands toward their wives. Even in the creation account, Adam didn't first see Eve as his submissive helper, but as his beautiful lover. Adam's first recorded words were a love poem, or maybe even a song, to Eve. Adam woke up to see that God had finished creation with something that he could never have imagined, and when he woke up and rubbed his eyes, he beheld Eve for the very first time and burst into song:

> *This at last is bone of my bones and flesh of my flesh; she shall be called Woman, because she was taken out of Man.* [12]

Every time I read this, I hear Etta James in the background—"At laassttt, my love has come along."[13] Adam's leadership and Eve's submission are grounded first in God's design and intent and second in their love and affection toward each other. Those who object most strongly toward patriarchy seem to imagine that the whole purpose of male headship was to suppress women, but Adam seems to view Eve differently when he exclaims, "At long last, here is another creature just like me."

Many scholars point out that these words could also be the very first marriage vows. In the ancient world, bones and flesh were often used poetically to suggest good times and bad. Adam wakes up, he lays

---

[12] Genesis 2:23
[13] James, Etta. "At Last." Argo Records, 1960.

eyes on the beautiful woman that God has created, and he exclaims, "bone of my bones and flesh of my flesh; she shall be called Woman." In other words, "Just as I am man, so now, in sickness and in health, she shall be called woman." No matter what comes, she and I are connected, and we will share the same name. Does this sound familiar? Consider this example of a traditional wedding vow often spoken by the bride and groom in wedding ceremonies:

> I take you to be my lawfully wedded husband/wife, to have and to hold from this day forward, for better or for worse, for richer or for poorer, in sickness and in health, to love and to cherish, until death do us part.

I know exactly how Adam felt; one of my favorite life memories is when I stood at the altar watching the doors of Mauldin First Baptist Church swing open and seeing Angela in her wedding gown for the first time. There she stood, more beautiful than I could have even imagined. As her dad walked her down the aisle, I cried (and she still makes fun of me for it). In that moment, we professed our love and commitment to one another. I promised to lead her; she promised to submit to me; but more than anything, we promised to love. I loved her more that day than I ever had, and because of my love for her, I was willing to do whatever I could to care for her. We didn't focus on our roles that day, nor have we felt the need to focus much attention on our roles in the days since. We love each other and we love Jesus, and because of our love, our marriage continues to be built up according to God's word.

The enemy has turned the tide on humanity by turning husbands against wives in a battle for authority and leadership. Rather than loving their wives as Christ loved his church, many men (even in the name of Christianity) have sought to exercise authority over their wives in the way that the rulers of the Gentiles lorded authority over their subjects. It was never God's intent for the husband to be the king of his little domain, but rather for the husband to be the lover and protector of his family. The home is not a castle for a husband to reign, but a cross where he dies daily in love and service toward his family. The family is a place of sacrifice for husbands.

> The home is not a castle for a husband to reign, but a cross where he dies daily in love and service toward his family. The family is a place of sacrifice for husbands.

Adam failed Eve when he chose to love his own comfort more than he loved protecting her from the evil one. This same sin is seen regularly in the homes of churched families when fathers choose their own comfort over the need for spiritual protection for their families. Rather than standing in the gap, praying for their wives and children, and leading spiritually in the home, many husbands and fathers are spiritually absent in the lives of their families. They retreat to their televisions and hobbies, surrendering the spiritual battle for their families to the evil one rather than engaging him with the power of the gospel. Men fail when they choose self-satisfaction over sacrifice.

Families do not have to fail, but too many fathers have thrown in the towel of leadership and love, taking up a soft banner of surrender. Rather than fighting for their families, husbands and fathers are content to allow the evil one to turn family members against one another without so much as a spiritual punch thrown. God's command is for husbands to love their wives and lead their families, and this will be done by following Christ's example. It was Christ who girded himself with a towel and washed the feet of his disciples. Christ hung on a cross to ransom sinners from their sentence of eternal death. His death on a cross was not an act of defeat but a declaration of war that resulted in his ultimate victory over sin.

Following his example, fathers should be serving their families generously and bravely. Fathers must lead in a way that does not alienate or belittle their children. Husbands should love so sacrificially that wives gladly and willingly follow their leadership. Only by living in the power of the Spirit can fathers lead spiritually and open avenues for the salvation of their families. Husbands must take the lead spiritually, praying with their wives and children, leading the family in church membership and attendance, and living lives of holiness that reflect the God who has given them their position of responsibility. In this context, women will find it easy and rewarding to follow their husbands and willingly submit to his leadership because they will find that his love creates a safe environment for their total trust. In safe and loving environments protected from many of life's stressors and dangers, women can blossom and grow. In this context, Satan will find it difficult to create a wedge where sin and division can fester because a spiritually disciplined family fights against his cunning and temptation.

Wives Loving Through Submission

Submission is hard because trust is hard. The Bible has commanded women to submit to their husbands, but this act of submission is not one that should open the door to abuse or degradation. Instead, this act of loving submission opens the door to God's blessings upon the family—his first institution for showing the world his love through real relationships. Contrary to the arguments of egalitarians, the Bible makes certain distinctions in the roles of marriage, but that does not equal a distinction in value. Both husband and wife are equally valuable to God and to each other because both have been created in the image of God and both are invited to be part of God's kingdom in Christ.

The distinction in roles is given as a guide to ensure happiness and fulfillment in marriage and to demonstrate to the world the kind of relationship that exists among the Trinity. Just as Father, Son, and Holy Spirit are equal in essence but distinct in their respective roles, so too, man and woman are equal in essence and personhood but have been given distinct roles in marriage.

Ladies, your responsibility within the marriage relationship is to ensure stability and success through loving submission to your husband. The role of extravagant lover and leader is given to the husband, not as a means of power, but as a responsibility to protect and provide for his wife. Submission, however, is not secondary to authority.

The role given to women is one of empowerment. Adam couldn't care for God's creation alone. He needed help. He needed a co-laborer. Rather than being satisfied to sit on the sidelines in their marriage relationship, women are called to be active participants in the loving relationship initiated by their husbands. Husbands are called to give themselves in service to their wives, and wives are called to reciprocate that love by empowering their husbands to love and excel even more in every area of life. In roles that mimic those of the Trinity, the husband should always be pointing to the wife as his helper, and the wife should always be pointing to the husband as her protective lover.

Far from being powerless, women can display leadership in the home by submitting to and supporting their husbands. For those who are willing to support their husbands in their vocation of Christian ministry, for instance, women can have more than their own ministry; they can also be co-laborers with their husbands; aiding in the efforts of bringing others to Christ.

Writing from a secular perspective, Stephen King recounts the love and support of his wife that enabled him to achieve success as a novelist.

> My wife made a crucial difference during those two years I spent teaching at Hampden (and washing sheets at New Franklin Laundry during the summer vacation). If she had suggested that the time I spent writing stories on the front porch of our rented house on Pond Street or in the laundry room of our rented trailer on Klatt Road in Hermon was wasted time, I think a lot of the heart would have gone out of me. Tabby never voiced a single doubt, however. Her support was a constant, one of the few good things I could take as a given. And whenever I see a first novel dedicated to a wife (or a husband), I smile and think, there's someone who knows. Writing is a lonely job. Having someone who believes in you makes a lot of difference. They don't

have to make speeches. Just believing is usually enough.[14]

The Bible shows that women can also be successful in bringing their husbands to faith in Christ by submitting to their leadership.

> *Likewise, wives, be subject to your own husbands, so that even if some do not obey the word, they may be won without a word by the conduct of their wives—when they see your respectful and pure conduct. Do not let your adorning be external—the braiding of hair, the wearing of gold, or the putting on of clothing—but let your adorning be the hidden person of the heart with the imperishable beauty of a gentle and quiet spirit, which in God's sight is very precious.*[15]

The real question that must be answered by wives is this: "What is most important?"

In God's economy, the family trumps personal accomplishments and achievements. In reality, what greater personal accomplishment should we recognize than a woman who raises kids well? The Bible does

> In God's economy, the family trumps personal accomplishments and achievements.

---

[14] King, Stephen. *On Writing: A Memoir of The Craft.* p. 64.
[15] 1 Peter 3:1-4

not say that women cannot or should not be successful on their own. In fact, it records many examples of successful women. The famous Proverbs 31 woman is portrayed as both enterprising and godly. She is strong and dignified, and by most standards, it appears that she would be considered successful in our world today. She worked outside the home and labored to serve her family well. She was respected and honored. But the key to her biblical renown is that her desire is first and foremost for her God and her family. This, of course, is not so different than the command given to husbands to love their wives. Marriages and families that overcome the attacks of the evil one do so because they have chosen to put God and family above personal gain or success.

Godly submission is not slavery, nor is it commanded only for those whose husbands exercise love as Christ does. Godly submission is a willing and obedient acquiescence to God's command. As shown in the passage from 1 Peter above, godly submission is commanded and expected from wives as an act of obedience to God, not an act of obedience to one's husband.

The Pride Problem

If the Bible is clear, and if God wants families to succeed, why do so many struggle? Why do husbands not love their wives as Christ loves his church and wives not submit to their husbands as Christ does to his Heavenly Father? Husbands and wives do not assume their proper roles within the marriage when they are content to live under the control of the Evil One who blinds lovers into believing that the individual self should rise above the married self. Rather than recognizing themselves as one organism united through God's activity, husband and wife continue to live and act as separate entities, each vying for their own personal gain, and the result is turmoil and marital destruction.

Families have bought the lie from culture and from the Father of Lies himself that personal gain trumps familial success. Climbing the corporate ladder is more important than maintaining a happy and Christ-centered home. Mothers are often not valued for their work in the home, while career women are idolized for their ability to juggle numerous responsibilities. The success of men is gauged, not by the spiritual well-being of their progeny and the satisfaction of their spouse, but by worldly standards of possessions and job security. The focus is so self-centered that the home is simply a launching pad for personal ambition rather than a center for a thriving family.

Happiness and joy cannot be found inside a context of overwhelming personal ambition. Philosopher Jennifer Frey has pointed out that those who describe themselves as happiest for the long haul are people whose lives are characterized by self-sacrifice.[16] For instance, many people choose not to have children because they don't want to be tied down. They believe that children will only get in the way of their happiness and contentment. However, just the opposite is true. People who have children consistently describe themselves as happier and more fulfilled than those who do not have children. In other words, the happiest people are those who find others to love and care for, not those who find excuses to prioritize their own well-being.

> The happiest people are those who find others to love and care for, not those who find excuses to prioritize their own wellbeing.

Someone once said that humility is not thinking less of yourself, but thinking of yourself less. In marriage, the pride problem is illustrated well by the fact that individuals think of themselves too often. Rather than thinking of their responsibilities to their spouse or children, partners in a marriage think of their own yearnings for personal fulfillment and temporal desires. In this line of thought, time with the guys trumps spiritual leadership, and a corner office is far superior to a happy Christ-centered home. If you don't believe it, consider that eight of the top ten reasons listed for

---

[16] https://humanize.today/2021/07/suffering-and-sacrifice-are-part-of-a-flourishing-human-life/.

divorce in one recent survey have to do with personal differences or desires for autonomy.[17]

In this environment stained by the fall, the man and woman do not live as one; instead, her desire is for her husband (or to have authority over her husband), and he rules over her (instead of leading her with the heart of Christ).[18] It was never God's intention for the husband and wife to be locked into a struggle for authority, but for them to live in harmony with one another and with God. It was humanity's sin against God that brought about this struggle, but it will not always be so. In C. S. Lewis's Chronicles of Narnia, the kingdom of Narnia thawed from its deep freeze when Aslan, the king, returned. As the long winter of Narnia thaws when Aslan is on the move, so too can we see the cycle of sin and pain beginning to break when God moves within families. Christ's redemptive work on the cross has set in motion the reversal of God's curse. The debt for Adam's sin has been paid, and husband and wife no longer have to struggle against one another while held captive to their sin. The gospel has set them free to live in Christ by loving and submitting to one another, just as the Father, Son, and Spirit relate to each other through love, leadership, and submission.

The pride of your individual success can be slain because Christ has set you free from your sin. The Great

---

[17] http://www.huffingtonpost.com/yourtango/10-most-common-reasons-people-divorce_b_8086312.html.
[18] Genesis 3:16

Rescue has taken place, and husbands and wives can claim the same victory as individuals and the church as a whole. The gospel of Jesus is enough to empower you to live out the commands of God and find joy in your marriage. You can live as one flesh without competition. You can experience your marriage as a happy partnership. You may have to sacrifice much of yourself, but you will gain even more of your spouse in the process. When you die to yourself in marriage, your success in marriage becomes a trophy for all the world to see. Even more important, when you die to yourself, Christ shines brightly, and your relationship becomes a witness to the world of Christ's work in your marriage and on your behalf. Fight the battle of sin in your marriage with confidence that the war has already been won, and see God use your marriage as a tool to proclaim his goodness and glory to those around you.

PRACTICAL APPLICATION

Family Cooking and Messy Kitchens

Love and relationships are built in the middle of life's messes and hassles. As you spend time together as a couple and as a family, you practically work out the realities of love, leadership, authority, submission, and family, with and for your kids.

Angela (my wife) makes homemade biscuits. Lots of biscuits. She has spoiled our family because she makes such good biscuits so regularly. On Saturday mornings when there are biscuits, the kitchen table can sometimes look like a disaster. Plates are piled high with biscuits and bacon. There is maple syrup, apple jelly, grape jelly, muscadine jelly, strawberry-fig preserves, Karo syrup, and butter. There is often cheese and occasionally even gravy.

We all gather around the table and pass biscuits, bacon, and condiments. The kids enjoy putting a jelly jar on the lazy Susan in the center of the table to spin it to whoever wants it next.

After breakfast, the kitchen is a wreck. There is a bread bowl to wash, bacon pans, at least six plates, cups, bowls, utensils, and the sticky table must be wiped and re-wiped.

Why in the world do we put ourselves through this on a Saturday morning?

One of the reasons, no doubt, is that Angela's most prominent spiritual gift is serving. She finds great joy in cooking for and serving her family. But the other reason is simply that we believe our family is better because we spend time around that table on Saturday mornings. As the kids get older, the Saturday morning ritual doesn't happen as often as it once did, but it is still just as wonderful every time it does.

Your kitchen is naturally one of the most *analog* rooms in your home. By analog, I mean not digital or computerized. Analog experiences are tactile and in-person. There are spoons, forks, and knives. Ovens are hot, refrigerators are cold. Water is wet, coffee is wonderful. Kitchens are filled with tastes, smells, sounds, touches, and beautiful sights to behold. Even the digital gadgets in your kitchen, like thermometers, only exist to help you in the process of an analog experience: cooking.

Kitchens are great places for families to grow together. Even the largest kitchen feels small when you have multiple people cooking. In those small spaces, you have the opportunity to practice healthy touch and use plenty of encouraging words.

When was the last time that you cooked something in the kitchen as a family? Remember, you do not have to be a gourmet chef to bake cookies with your kids. Anyone can follow a recipe. You can even take shortcuts and buy cookie mixes or pre-made cookie dough.

Kitchens become places where amazing things can happen. Important conversations take place because your kids don't have to look you in the eye. Sometimes, it is easier to have hard conversations when you are shoulder-to-shoulder with someone rather than seated face-to-face. When you are elbow deep in washing dishes, your kids will sometimes feel more comfortable talking about the tough things at school, relationship problems, or even bullying.

Kitchens are also places to redeem time for conversations. If you are always in the kitchen by yourself, you are missing out on hours per week that could be redeemed with important and intentional conversation. Maybe your kids aren't old enough to help in the kitchen yet, but they just want to be near you when you work. How can you accomplish that? Let them color a picture at the table while you prepare dinner. Give them a puzzle to work on while you wash dishes, or let them do their homework in the same room where you are frying eggs.

There is so much good that can come from your kids spending time in the kitchen.

Healthy Eating

As your kids work in the kitchen, they learn the value of healthy foods. Kids are naturally curious, and when they are in the kitchen, they read labels. At some point in their lives, every one of our kids has asked, "What are calories?" Our explanation has always been the same: "Calories are a measure of how much energy is contained in food."

Once they have been equipped with this knowledge, they begin reading packages to see how many calories are in everything. EVERYTHING.

"Dad, do you know how many calories are in those M&M'S?" *(No, and I don't want to know right now while I am sneaking a snack before dinner...)*

Their curiosity doesn't stop with calories. We get to talk about protein, salt, sugar intake, and hydration.

When they make sweet tea, for instance, kids see how much sugar goes into that one pitcher of colored water.

Of course, getting kids to prefer cabbage over macaroni and cheese is not a given, but when kids help in the kitchen, they are usually eager to eat what they helped to prepare. One of our children went through a stage where he refused to eat scrambled eggs. We eat lots of eggs, so this was an inconvenience for the entire family.

One evening, Angela planned to prepare breakfast for dinner (because there were leftover biscuits!). She was picking up other kids from practices, so I finished dinner. The kid who didn't like scrambled eggs wanted to help me crack eggs and stir them. When everyone sat down at the table, he proudly explained that he had made the eggs, and you can probably guess what happened next. Suddenly, he loved scrambled eggs.

Will your kids unexpectedly fall in love with Brussels sprouts if they help to cook them? Maybe not, but they will be more excited to try them if they cook them. In the kitchen, you can teach your kids what they should eat and why, and if they come alongside you in the kitchen, they are more open to trying new things.

Life Skills

My mom was terrified that I would marry someone who couldn't cook. She didn't want me to starve. I'm convinced that it was her fear that caused her to teach my brothers and me basic culinary skills.

When you spend time in the kitchen with your kids, they learn valuable life skills. Everyone needs to know how to cook an egg, cut an onion, bake chicken, and boil water. But think beyond the basics.

> When you spend time in the kitchen with your kids they learn valuable life skills.

In the kitchen, you teach math skills. Kids learn to measure, to multiply their measurements, and even to divide them. Reading the back of a pancake mix box often requires rudimentary math. If 6 servings of pancakes require ¾ cup of pancake mix and 18 servings require 2 ¼ cups of pancake mix, how much pancake mix is needed for 12 servings?

Kids learn how to handle hot things with oven mitts and how hot things can even burn countertops. The kitchen teaches how to handle a knife and, occasionally, how to sharpen a knife—the knife sharpeners in our kitchen drawers seem to attract kids like a magnet. In the kitchen, kids learn how to wash dishes, how to sweep a floor, and how to clean up after themselves.

You can also teach basic manners in the kitchen. Most of the time, you are bumping into each other and jockeying for the same space in a kitchen. Even in those moments, words like "excuse me," "please," and "thank you" begin to become ingrained.

Confidence

Of course, there are more complex and impressive skills to be learned in the kitchen along with the basics. In the kitchen, you learn how to trim a whole brisket, how to marinate a steak, or how to bake a cake. My daughter makes an excellent pound cake. She has taken the time to learn how to make it, and as a result, she doesn't just make a good cake for a kid; she makes a cake that her family fights over.

Kitchens are great places to teach, because everything is hands-on. When you teach your kid how to handle a hot pan, you do it by showing them, then helping them, and then finally watching them do it properly. When you teach a child to grill burgers, they learn how to pat out the meat, how to season the meat, how to light a grill, how to clean a grill, and even how to keep the dog from burning its mouth on the hot burger they dropped on the deck.

Every aspect of learning in the kitchen requires teaching and hands-on instruction, along with quick feedback. Kids practice football for weeks before they play a game and learn if they are any good. Piano recitals only come around once or twice each year. But it only takes about thirty minutes from start to finish to grill burgers for dinner. Each time your kids cook, they learn a little more, they get a little better, and they grow more confident in their abilities.

Service

Richard Foster opens his chapter on the spiritual discipline of service this way: "As the cross is the sign of submission, so the towel is the sign of service."[1] When Jesus gathered with his disciples for the Last Supper, he did so wrapped in a towel. The disciples had been arguing over who was the greatest, but Jesus knelt before them and washed their feet with these words, "If I then, your Lord and Teacher, have washed your feet, you also ought to wash one another's feet. For I have given you an example, that you also should do just as I have done to you."[2]

In the kitchen, your children will learn many things, but perhaps most importantly, they can learn the spiritual discipline of service. There are opportunities for service in every corner of a kitchen. Meal preparation is a service for the family, but so is washing dishes, wiping tables, and sweeping floors.

Jesus's disciples argued over who was the greatest,[3] and they wanted to rule in the coming kingdom.[4] But

---

[1] Foster, Richard. *Celebration of Discipline*. p. 126.
[2] John 13:14-15
[3] Luke 9:46
[4] Matthew 20:21

the way of Christ is different. He worked to redirect their desires,

> *"You know that the rulers of the Gentiles lord it over them, and their great ones exercise authority over them. It shall not be so among you. But whoever would be great among you must be your servant, and whoever would be first among you must be your slave, even as the Son of Man came not to be served but to serve, and to give his life as a ransom for many."[5]*

Just as Jesus's first disciples were commanded to serve, so too are the young disciples you are raising in your home. Service is an important Christian discipline. As a parent, you get to teach your children to serve others through your local church or by volunteering in your community. But do not miss the daily opportunity to teach the discipline of service in the kitchen. The daily, uncelebrated aspects of kitchen duties create a wonderful laboratory for your kids to learn to serve as Jesus commanded.

---

[5] Matthew 20:25-28

CHAPTER THREE

The Challenge of Commitment

Therefore, a man shall leave his father and mother and hold fast to his wife, and the two shall become one flesh.

Ephesians 5:31

The couple that sat in my office was honest. I was

their last hope, and if I couldn't help them work through the problems in their marriage, they were going to get a divorce. We prayed, and I listened. I listened to pain and hurt, anger, and even rage. I heard his sins and her sins. He accused, and she cried. She accused, and he fumed. And then, I heard it. The real reason they were here.

> "I don't like the way he always sides with his mother or his brother over me. They seem to come first...always."

> "Well, I don't know what she expects me to do. They're family; I'm not going to turn my back on my family for her! Even when they're wrong. You know, preacher, they're still family."

> "See what I mean? That's how he always is. I don't want him to ignore his family, but what about me?"

Did you catch it? Did you see the major problem in the marriage? Mothers, brothers, sisters, and cousins are family, and you must stick with family. Somehow, the two partners in this marriage had missed one of the most important commands from God concerning marriage. Interestingly, it is also one of the first commands given by God when he institutes the covenant of marriage, all the way back in Genesis 2:24. Paul says it in Ephesians

5:31, but he is only echoing the command of God from the beginning of time.

> *Therefore, a man shall leave his father and his mother and hold fast to his wife, and they shall become one flesh.*

To put it a little more bluntly, the wife becomes the family of the husband, and the husband becomes the family of the wife. The couple in my office had apparently entered their marriage in a way that more resembles a business agreement than a biblical covenant. They weren't committed to each other as family members who had to work through their differences. They didn't see a blood connection; they only saw a transactional and disposable relationship. Their thoughts may have gone something like this:

> "I can't do anything about being related to my brother, but I can end this relationship with my wife (or husband)."

Biblically, the marriage covenant is something far greater than a blood relationship. Marriage and its consummation bring husband and wife into a union that is stronger than blood. They do not have a close ancestor that binds them together; instead, they literally become one person. I once heard a pastor explain the marriage union well during a wedding rehearsal. He looked at the soon-to-be husband and wife and said this, "Timothy, tomorrow, you will cease to exist, and Janelle, you will cease as well." Instead, they became Timothy-Janelle and Janelle-Timothy. They both retained their individual personalities, but at the time of their marriage, they became more together as a couple than they were before as individuals. They were joined together, and now they pursue Jesus together as husband and wife and as parents. All these years later, they seem to be more joined together today than they were then.

So, what did the couple in my office need, and what do thousands, perhaps millions, of other couples across the United States and around the world need? They need a fresh and strong commitment to one another. Commitment is one of the greatest spiritual victories needed in marriage today. The forces of darkness around us will do all they can to destroy commitment in a marriage. The Father of Lies will be very convincing. The couple in my office had bought the lie that they were not really related to each other. Sure, they were married, but that was different.

> Commitment is one of the greatest spiritual victories needed in marriage today.

Satan is satisfied when this kind of attitude is pervasive in marriage relationships. When the marriage relationship is seen as disposable, driving a wedge between husband and wife is easy. Adultery is inviting when there is no real commitment, and time with one's spouse is not necessary when commitment goes no deeper than the surface. Marriages that stand the test of time do so because the level of commitment from both parties approaches the level of supernatural.

What does this commitment between husband and wife look like? Simply, the husband leaves his father and mother and clings to his wife, and the wife leaves behind her father and mother to cling to her husband. There must be a separation from the old and a union with the new. Your father's and/or mother's household can no longer be the driving factor in your family decisions. Biblical commitment within the confines of marriage means that your entire family structure must be redefined. You still love your momma, but she's not in charge. There is a new household made up of husband and wife, and the old household must be left in the old house. But how can you get there?

Overcoming the Obstacles to Commitment

The climate of the twenty-first century is not one that lends itself well to the concept of marital commitment and fidelity. The hook-up and shack-up culture of the United States is the clearest indicator of the prevailing mood of non-commitment that exists in our culture. The number of cohabitations has risen dramatically over the past thirty years and is even celebrated in the media.[1] Cohabitating creates an opportunity for those who want to play house with no strings attached. The problem with cohabitation, aside from the social ills that are regularly noted,[2] is that it is unbiblical to the core. Although contemporary culture has become increasingly tolerant of this practice, the Christian worldview must remain especially vigilant in this area. God's design for sexual relationships is characterized by commitment and fidelity in biblical marriage.

> The problem with cohabitation, aside from the social ills noted, is that it is unbiblical to the core.

Easy sex with no expectation of obligation or faithfulness on the part of millions of single people has become a huge obstacle to commitment. This obstacle will not be overcome with more attention to social science and pop psychology. Only the power of the gospel working in the hearts and minds of believers will bring about changed attitudes toward commitment in relationships. "Hooking up" and "shacking up" cause

---

[1] A USA Today article from 2008 shows that the number of cohabitating couples has risen dramatically in the past thirty years and that the opinion of the American culture as it relates to this practice has gone from negative to positive. Interestingly, though the polling date from USA Today shows that people do not believe that cohabitation leads to higher divorce rates, the article did not support a single study to add weight to this point. The article can be accessed at http://www.usatoday.com/news/nation/census/2008-07-28-cohabitation-census_N.htm

[2] For example, see article by Virginia Wing, "The Truth About Domestic Violence in Marital Verses Cohabitational Relationships" at http://www.citizenlink.org/FOSI/marriage/cohabitation/A000000890.cfm

issues with commitment, but there are other temptations in our culture that also create problems.

Match.com, a popular dating site, once had as its slogan, "It's okay to look." This same slogan has created a huge obstacle to commitment within marriage relationships. Somehow our culture has embraced pornography as normal and acceptable; even within many marriages, husbands and wives have decided that it is OK to look as long as you don't touch. This is not a biblical concept, and it is a huge hindrance to total commitment within marriage. It was Jesus, after all, who said that lusting is equal to committing adultery. Looking at naked or near-naked images of someone other than your husband or wife destroys commitment within the marriage. Watching others perform sex acts for personal gratification erodes trust and intimacy within marriage. Run from the wisdom of the world on this issue. Pornography is cancer to commitment.

But, of course, lust does not happen only through looking at visual pornography. Pornography can be read on the printed page of filthy romance novels as well. Women are especially susceptible to this temptation. The preponderance of e-readers and audiobooks has made the consumption of literary smut nearly as private as online porn because no one knows what you're reading on that Kindle. Rather than finding contentment in the arms of their husbands through committed relationships, some women fulfill their fantasies vicariously through the pages of romance novels, just as some husbands do through the clicks of their mouse on porn websites. As Christians, we must stand against pornography and other lustful addictions that are cancerous to commitment within marriage.

As an aside, one huge obstacle to commitment in marriages often comes on the night before the wedding day. If you are reading this before you get married, please pay attention. Bachelor and bachelorette parties, though thought of as the last hoorah for a friend before the big day, often slide headfirst into sin and shame. Strip clubs, drunken romps at nightclubs, and who-knows-what-else can plant the seed of non-commitment just hours before the couple-to-be says their "I do's." If you plan to be committed to one person for all your life, then do not put yourself in a situation that may compromise that commitment. Engagement and eventual marriage carry with it a commitment to ONE person. Any situation into which you enter willingly that causes you to be tempted to focus your sexual attention toward a person other than your fiancé or spouse is dangerous and inconsistent with a Christian understanding of commitment and marriage.

Russian roulette is a bad idea. Sure, you spin the barrel and you have a five in six chance of living, but you also have a one in six chance of dying. Sowing your wild oats for just one last night with "the guys" or "the girls" may have a chance of being raunchy fun without any lasting damage, but why would you throw the dice on your marriage? Why put your marriage at risk by indulging in porn or strip clubs or raunchy romance novels, or embarrassingly distasteful bachelor and bachelorette parties? The way of Christ is better. Christians must flee from the cultural norms that allow and even encourage these obstacles to commitment.

Experiencing the Freedom of Commitment

Commitment, although not always easy and not always celebrated in the public sphere, allows married couples a certain freedom that they do not and cannot otherwise enjoy. When both parties in the marriage relationship have confidence that the other has left their old life and is clinging to their spouse for their married life, they can fully trust and enjoy one another in every way. 1 Corinthians 7:4 says, "For the wife does not have authority over her own body, but the husband does. Likewise, the husband does not have authority over his own body, but the wife does." 1 Corinthians 7 speaks directly to couples in regard to their sexual relationship. This will be addressed in greater detail in chapter five of this book, but for now, note that for a wife to give authority of her body to her husband and a husband to trust the authority over his body to his wife, the relationship must be one that is characterized by complete and total commitment. There are great benefits from commitment in the marriage relationship, and a great sex life is just one.

Paul's words to the Corinthians are about more than sex. Husband and wife are to come together sexually so that they will not be tempted. A married couple's commitment to each other through regular sexual relations serves to protect their relationship from Satan's advances.

Committed couples enjoy greater levels of happiness together. In their book, *Saving Your Marriage Before It Starts*, Drs. Les and Leslie Parrott have this to say about commitment and happiness. "The trick is to develop the right attitude in spite of the circumstances we find ourselves in...happy couples decide to be happy. In spite of the troubles life deals them, they make happiness a habit."[3] They go on to say, "Happiness in marriage has nothing to do with luck and everything to do with will."[4] Happy couples are not necessarily perfect, and their happiness is not always the result of an easy marriage. Every marriage has its own unique set of problems. But happy marriages are composed of individuals who have decided, above all else, that they are committed to one another, and come hell or high water, they will stay married, PERIOD. The Parrots,

---
[3] Parrott, Drs. Les and Leslie. *Saving Your Marriage Before It Starts.* p. 60.
[4] Ibid. p 61

again, say it like this. "Research reveals that the level of a couple's joy is determined by each partner's ability to adjust to things beyond his or her control. Every happy couple has learned to find the right attitude in spite of the conditions they find themselves in." [5]

Committed couples also experience a higher degree of trust and individual freedom than non-committed couples. My wife tells a story about a high-school friend who liked to spend her weekend nights away from her boyfriend, driving around to see where he was. She didn't trust him, so she wasted time checking on him, infringing on his "guy-time" and ruining any chance she had at quality time with her girlfriends. Obviously, this is just a silly high school relationship, but many marriages never get beyond this obstacle. Apps like Find My iPhone have made this sort of stalking easier, and I have seen it even rob married couples of joy and trust. If your level of trust is so low in your marriage that you need to call your spouse and ask, "Why are you at Target?" there are greater issues in your relationship than the money being spent on the popcorn combo in the Target cafe. *(Side note: For those who are not aware, before COVID-19 robbed us of this joy, Target stores had a small café that sold excellent popcorn at a reasonable price, perfect for eating as you walked around and watched your wife shop.) The world is worse because Target cafes no longer exist.)*

---

[5] Ibid. p. 66.

I once met a guy who had given up hunting and fishing because when he came home with an empty cooler, his wife assumed that he had been cheating on her instead of spending a day in the woods. Fortunately for me, Angela does not struggle with that kind of paranoia, because my time in the woods often proves why it is called hunting and not killing. If she accused me of lying every time I came home from the woods empty-handed, I would be in a real mess.

Non-committed couples know nothing of trust and security in a relationship. As a result, those relationships are often unhealthy. Marriages characterized by strong commitment, however, have developed a level of trust and security that enables both partners to live individual lives free of the intrusion of their spouse. So, a wife can spend a weekend with the girls without her husband freaking out in jealousy, and a husband can take a day for fishing without his insecure wife calling every ten minutes to make sure he's still on the lake. When couples are committed, they learn to trust each other. In trusting relationships, Satan's advances are more easily repelled. The devil struggles to find a foothold in happy marriages.

> The devil struggles to find a foothold in happy marriages.

The freedoms of commitment do not come because marriage is perfect. "Marriages can never be perfect because people are not perfect... Living happily ever after only works when you make it work."[6] The "work" of marriage begins with a commitment to the marriage above all else. When both parties are committed, first and foremost, to Christ and to the success of marriage, living happily ever after has a chance because the couple is at least determined to make it work together.

Trust God's Word and Fight for Commitment

All the powers of hell seem to fight against commitment. One of the most heartbreaking experiences of my life was a conversation with a guy at the gym who had given up on commitment to his wife and kids. He heard a whisper from the pit of hell and bought the lie as truth. He believed that by being committed to his wife and kids, he was robbing himself of the pleasure and satisfaction that could be found in the arms of other women. He truly believed that there were many women in the world who would be eager to hook up with him if he could only shed the commitment he had to his family. He craved the attention of women, and Satan convinced him that his wife was the obstacle. Rather than finding joy in the wife of his youth, he wanted to find pleasure with other women.

If Satan can convince you that your spouse is the obstacle to your happiness, you will begin to fight

---
[6] Ibid. 74-75.

against your spouse. In believing the lie, commitment to your spouse will no longer be a source of joy and fulfillment, but a hindrance. You must fight against this lie with the truths of God's word. Proverbs 18:22 says, "He who finds a good wife finds a good thing and obtains favor from the Lord." God's word says that your wife is good and is a blessing. Satan says that your wife is an obstacle and a hindrance.

My friend Buster is the senior adult pastor at our church. In a staff meeting, he once said that he was amazed that after more than forty years of marriage, it seems as though his relationship with his wife gets better every day. Those words spoke volumes to me. For those of us early in our marriages who think it can't get any better, there is always a senior advisor to point out that it has only just begun. The fruits of commitment in marriage will long outlast youthful passions and vitality. But commitment early on will fertilize the root system of a marriage that will produce long-lasting fruit for years to come. Commitment lays the groundwork for spiritual victory within your family.

> The fruits of commitment in marriage will long outlast youthful passions and vitality.

So work now to fertilize and cultivate your marriage, laying the groundwork for a strong root system that will yield an abundant crop. Take these suggestions below, and maybe add some of your own, as ways to improve your marriage and cultivate your commitment to your spouse.

1. Plan a regular date night.
2. Dream together.
3. Share your victories, struggles, and defeats with your spouse.
4. Play together.
5. Eat dinner as a family as often as possible.
6. Surprise your spouse with gifts.
7. Make long-term plans for an exotic vacation.
8. Celebrate anniversaries.

Commitment is not an easy course to navigate early in marriage. In fact, the land mines and obstacles to commitment will be many, and the grass will often seem greener on the other side of the fence. One thing I've always noticed, however, is that the grass is greenest in my yard where my favorite German Shorthaired Pointers (the world's greatest dogs) do their business. When we are tempted to believe lies, we must claim truth. All truth is God's truth, and there is victory in truth. The lies of greener pastures often conceal the truth about organic fertilizers that can ruin your shoes. So, when you are looking over your neighbor's fence for the greener pasture that may provide escape from the mundane commitments of your marriage, just remember what you will be stepping into and, instead opt for the hard work of commitment for the long run.

PRACTICAL APPLICATION

Tablecloths

One aspect of leaving your family of origin and clinging to your spouse is creating your own household with your own family and your own family traditions.

> Cling to your spouse and create your own household with your own family traditions.

No longer do the rules of your parents create the culture. This new family is comprised of a committed husband and wife who, together, create a new culture in their home.

There is a buffet drawer in

our foyer filled with tablecloths. I don't know how many there are, but I'm sure there are more than five. There are all different sizes and shapes of tablecloths. I know we have a green one and one has snowflakes. One isn't even a tablecloth at all; it is a table runner.

To be honest, tablecloths in our house are for guests, special occasions, and anytime we eat at the dining room table instead of the kitchen table—just like Angela and I learned in the homes where we grew up. Our kitchen table is filled with scratches, scrapes, and homework scars. The dining room table is regularly polished and decorated. Tablecloths on the dining room table serve two purposes: they enhance the beauty of the table, and they protect it.

There is a good chance that if you come to my house for dinner, you will find a tablecloth on the dining room table. If you peek under that tablecloth, you will find a pad underneath that protects the table. That pad is pretty special, and only special guests get to see the table pad.

The table pad used to be white. Now you would say it is more like a white canvas upon which our kids have projected their artwork for fifteen years. The table pad is covered in marker, paint, pen marks, and probably Play-Doh crumbs, but a few years ago, I noticed something else.

On our formerly white table pad is the outline of a picture frame. It is obvious that the table pad was the backdrop for an intense crafting session where the paint ran off the edges of the picture frame. But, in the outline of that picture frame, written in perfect handwriting, are these words, "Picture frames with Brooke."

Brooke is our kids' former babysitter and one of our favorite people on the planet. When I saw that inscription, I snapped a quick picture and texted it to Brooke and her husband, and accused her of plastering our table protector with graffiti. But I was wrong. Brooke didn't write her name; one of our kids wrote her name in the margin of a messy craft as a reminder. Our kids wanted to remember the day they painted with Brooke, so they memorialized their mess with a Sharpie.

What does that story have to do with anything? If you come to my house, you will probably not see that table pad. You will see a tablecloth, but you will have no idea of the memories plastered underneath your plate. The tablecloth you see will serve as a reminder to you that you mattered enough for us to make you feel at home.

But if you are a certain kind of person—someone with a certain degree of familiarity in our home, you won't actually get a tablecloth. You will get something better. You'll be served (or maybe you'll serve yourself) on the table pad. On that pad, you will see Brooke's name and Aubrey's handwriting. You'll see Sloan's fingerprints and Brooklyn's creativity. You might even see a place where Wyatt colored outside the lines or where Angela spilled some glitter.

Certain people walk into our home, and they aren't greeted with tablecloths to cover our messes and scars. Those people walk into our home and are met with memories and messes. Brooke might never get served on a tablecloth in our home, because when she is with us, I always want to be reminded that she loved our kids enough to make little messes and create memories.

Brooke has her own son now, and I trust she will make the same kind of memories with him as he grows—maybe I'll even get to personalize a table pad in her home one day as I make memories with her kids.

The effort to turn our houses into homes comes in starts and stops, and it is filled with mistakes and messes. I write of a tablecloth, but I could mention cracked glasses or chipped sheetrock. Our boys share a bedroom complete with an indoor basketball goal and makeshift baseball games. One day, they'll grow up and I'll have to repair some sheetrock and repaint the ceiling, but until then, if you come into our home, you'll be reminded that boys live in that room, and they live loud.

This is the privilege you have as a family—and it can be one of the greatest challenges. In your home, you get to create the traditions, you get to choose

> In your home, you get to create the traditions. You must fight for your own unique culture.

the table coverings, and you must fight for your own unique culture. Your home should be uniquely yours—the kind of place that embodies your values and that helps you to shape your children. Your home should be analog in the best sense of the word—warm, inviting, comfortable, and culture-creating—and it should be a tactile extension of you and your spouse.

> God has called you to build your home for his glory and the good of the world and your family.

In your home, you get to decide the rules. You may allow running in the house, or dogs in the bed. You can choose whether shoes will be worn inside, and you can set bedtimes. As you make your house a home—a place of comfort, refuge, and growth for your family, you even get to decide if writing on a table pad is an activity to be punished or celebrated. That is sort of the point. It is the home God has given to you and that he has called you to build for his glory and the good of the world and your family.

Happy homes will often be far from pristine. I have a friend who has a house filled with beautiful artifacts and antiques, and taxidermy from all over the world. He also keeps his house filled with his grandkids and any other children who want to stop by. It terrifies me when my kids walk past the crystal or the stuffed bear. But he encourages

> Happy homes will often be far from pristine.

them to touch everything and ask questions. His house could be a museum, but instead it is a laboratory for love and learning. And it is wonderful.

You get to choose what you want your home to be. Do you have couches where no one is allowed to sit, or does your furniture exist to make people comfortable? Have you created spaces where your kids, or grandkids or neighbors can be creative and cozy? Do you want a home that could be featured on magazine covers, or do you want a home where memories are made and kept?

> What choices will you make to create the home of your dreams?

If you can't have both (and you probably can't), which one will you choose, and what choices will you make to create the home of your dreams?

CHAPTER FOUR

The Battle for Your Children

I love my children. I love and have loved them at all ages, but the process of transitioning from two to four kids was very challenging. In fact, that process amplified a truth that parents often deny: Raising children does not always feel like a blessing.

I recently sat in the home of weary parents who had bought into the lie that they were all alone and somehow the exception. They really believed no one else struggled with parenting. I was surprised when they said, "Wow, you are so honest." They had been deceived into believing all the social media posts and positive parenting comments about how wonderful raising children is.

Consider this: social media is narcissistic by definition. No one (myself included) tells all the ugly truths about their lives on Twitter. If you are a parent reading this book, I want to urge you to get away from social media and get social with your parenting. Talk with real parents who share your worldview and who are having real struggles, and you may be surprised by what you discover. Parenting is a team sport. First and foremost, your parenting team includes your spouse, but it should also extend beyond your household. You need a community of faith as a part of your parenting team.

Parenting is spiritual warfare. In the process of raising children, you are fighting your flesh, their flesh, the world around you, and all the forces of evil for the souls of your children. In fact, when a sleepless night turns into six

> Parenting is spiritual warfare. Losing your children is not an option. You must fight.

months of sleepless nights, it can seem as though you are fighting for your own soul as well. But losing your children to the world is not an option. You must fight.

A friend who is also a pastor looked at me during our adoption and said, "Wow, Craig, what you guys are doing is so awesome. You must feel so blessed every day." My reply: "No, we feel like we are in a war zone." Our difficulty was intensified by kids who came from abandonment and neglect and were scarred as a result, but it is not only foster care and adoption that can sometimes make parenting feel more like a burden than a blessing. Parents of wayward teens, single parents, and parents of children with special needs understand the daily struggle. Even parents of precious newborn babies learn that parenting is a blessing and a burden when their bundle of joy refuses to sleep.

But the news is not all bad.

The good news that many parents can attest to is that after months of struggle and strife, the blessings begin to show—babies start sleeping, parents adjust, behaviors regulate, sickness abates, and the joy of our children returns. However, the reality is that raising kids is difficult. Sometimes, toddlers feel more like terrorists sent to destroy our happy lives than blessings from above. If you are in a happy place with your kids right now and doubt this reality, just remember potty-training, or that kid who didn't sleep through the night for four years, or lice...and we haven't even made it to the teenage years.

But what can you do when the feeling of dread overwhelms your joy and satisfaction? How can you fight for joy in parenting when sin, Satan, or the world threatens to sap you of the delight that is to be found in your children? Here are some helpful steps:

1. **Be honest about your situation.** You don't have to share the gory details, but it is okay, and usually helpful, to share with others in your trusted community that your two-year-old is having temper tantrums or your sixteen-year-old got drunk last weekend. Scripture commands us to bear one another's burdens,[1] so rely on your church family and other believers. Honestly share your struggles and allow the people around you to minister to you. But it isn't only with others that you should be honest. Be honest when you go to God's word. Turn to God's word when you are broken and weary and trust it to meet you at the point of your need. You won't often receive God's help until you acknowledge that you need it.

2. **Run to Christ.** There is strength and life in reading God's word, even when it is hard to make time for it or you can't seem to hold your eyes open to read. His word reveals Christ, and he is your hiding place.[2] When parenting becomes overwhelming and you lose sight of the help that is found around you, never lose sight

---
[1] Galatians 6:2
[2] Psalm 32:7

of the help that is found in Christ. When your teenager rebels, don't waste your restless nights. Run to Christ. He is a friend who sticks closer than a brother, and his grace is sufficient for you,[3] even in the most difficult days of parenting.

3. **Name the enemy.** The family is one of the epicenters of spiritual warfare in our world, but your kids and your spouse are not the enemy. Satan is the enemy of your family and of your marriage. As we saw in the first chapter of this book, creation fell when Satan successfully created division between Adam and Eve. Their sin separated them from God and each other, but the sin had its ultimate root in Satan. The struggles in your family and your feelings of depression and defeat are not from Jesus. His yoke is easy and his burden is light,[4] but the whispers of Satan urge you to give up and walk away. Name the true enemy and then call on the name of Jesus, who has overcome. Satan is the enemy, but Christ is the victor. He has overcome sin, death, hell, and the grave. Satan is a defeated foe, and Jesus is your great hope.

4. **Be thankful.** In the most difficult times

---

[3] 2 Corinthians 12:9
[4] Matthew 11:30

of parenting, writing down a few things I was thankful for in my journal each day helped reshape my thoughts and feelings. Journaling is an important spiritual discipline, especially when the world around you seems to be caving in. For instance, you'd be amazed at how your perspective changes when you thank God for the strong will of your daughter, who will one day be responsible for your care in a nursing home. By reflecting on the blessings you have received in Christ, you can work to dig out of the pit of despair.

5. **Get help.** There is no shame in seeking counseling. Your pastor or other counselors can help you manage your feelings and emotions, and help you consider parenting techniques you may not have tried. Angela and I are both counselors, but at one point, counseling was invaluable for us. A good counselor helped us to view our parenting from the outside and to reconsider the best techniques to shepherd our children.

6. **Find an outlet.** Parenting is hard, and kids can be frustrating, so find an appropriate outlet for your stress and frustration. Strength training is my primary stress relief, so when life is hard, I go pick up heavy things at the gym. Maybe you

run, fish, or spend time hiking, go shoot guns, can fresh fruits, or work in your garden. Whatever you do, manage your stress.

7. **Don't be a martyr.** Seriously, you are not the only hope for your kids—Jesus is. Killing yourself does not prove to anyone that you are a better mother or father. Allowing someone else to help you may seem like a sign of weakness, but we are all vulnerable in some way. Send the kids to grandma. Let them go to a church event or stay late at school. Accept help from a friend who wants to come clean your house or watch your kids. Jesus died so that you wouldn't have to, and that applies to your parenting, too.

Yes, parenting is hard, and it brings all sorts of challenges from potty training to night terrors to teenage drama. Parenting is not for the faint of heart; however, when your cute toddler (or fourth grader or teenager) becomes a terror in your home, there is hope. Your kids may not seem like a sign of God's favor today, but trust in God's word and know that even when they do not seem to be a blessing, "Children are a heritage from the Lord, the fruit of the womb a reward."[5]

So, parents of little terrorists, take heart. God's word is always true. God designed the family for our good

---
[5] Psalm 127:3

and His glory. It is his plan for you to raise children who honor you and fear him, and, because it is God's plan, he has made it possible. As hard as it is to believe at times, there is hope in the spiritual struggle of raising children. Trust the Lord.

Don't Crowdsource Your Parenting

Take God at his word, but also take God's people to heart. Take a team approach, but don't crowdsource. There is a fine line between being honest about your situation and throwing your kids under a bus (figuratively, of course). Parenting is not your struggle against your kids. You are struggling alongside your kids against the sin that so easily entangles all of us. Love them through their struggles, and as you love them, take a team approach as a family and as a church family.

A team approach to raising your children is not the same as crowdsourcing. Crowdsourcing, according to Merriam-Webster, is "the practice of obtaining needed services, ideas, or content by soliciting contributions from a large group of people and especially from the online community rather than from traditional employees or suppliers." It is a relatively new phenomenon and one that has great merit in certain situations. One of my favorite crowdsourcing campaigns

> A team approach to raising your children is not the same as crowdsourcing.

was for the Coolest Cooler. Honestly, this cooler looks amazing. It has a blender, lights, charging ports, wheels, and speakers. Interestingly, the Kickstarter campaign was for funding, not for design ideas. Apparently, the folks who dreamed up the Coolest Cooler were happy to take your money, but they didn't want random people giving design input.

Unfortunately, I see crowdsourcing taking a very negative turn through social media. Many people are using their Facebook, Twitter, and Instagram pages as a sort of crowdsource parenting (or marriage) platform. Crowdsourcing has its place and is obviously a neat idea for fundraising or market research, but it is a terrible place for you to turn for advice on loving your spouse or raising your kids.

Crowdsourcing your parenting advice is a bad idea, first and foremost, because you need real community. The online community is a sort of reality, but it cannot replace face-to-face encounters with people you know. Do you want to know how to discipline your child? Turn to someone who has firsthand knowledge of both you and your child. Perhaps those who know you best recognize that the issue is not the form of discipline, but the person enforcing the discipline. That is a hard truth, but no one reading your four-sentence description on Facebook has actually witnessed your kid throwing a tantrum—or you losing your temper. You need real biblical community, not the pseudo-community of social media that only sees the side of you that you willingly share. You need to be advised by those who have seen all sides of you and can serve to show you what you need to see, and also serve as a mirror to reflect your actions back to you.

> You need real biblical community, not the pseudo-community of social media that only sees the side of you that you willingly share.

Second, crowdsourcing is a bad idea because you need advice from those who share your worldview. Crowdsourcing, by definition, obtains ideas through non-traditional sources. Your church is a very traditional source, and within a healthy community of believers, you will find people who share your worldview. Imagine, for example, your brown-eyed son doesn't want to eat his broccoli. Your Facebook friends may suggest covering it in cheese or discreetly baking it into a dessert (which sounds like a greater punishment than eating the broccoli all by itself!) because they believe that healthy eating is what matters most. However, those who share your worldview may understand that refusing broccoli is not only a dietary issue, but also a pride issue, revealing the rebellious heart of your two-year-old. Eating the broccoli is not only about health; it is about him learning to trust that mom and dad know best and have his best interest in mind. Ultimately, his ability and willingness to trust his parents will have ramifications on the way he views his relationship with God. Yes, making your child eat broccoli can be a form of spiritual warfare.

In all honesty, most of the crowdsourcing I see online for parents has nothing to do with how to raise a child to fear the Lord. It has to do with "mommy needs wine" or with how many glasses of wine are needed to make it through a day with a middle schooler, or how your local schoolteacher is the reason that your child can't read, or how the Democrats are to blame for your child's dismal future, or that the Republicans are literally killing your kids. Or, my favorite, the "expert" who has read all the blogs and knows exactly why you shouldn't vaccinate because an ex-Playboy model says it is a bad idea. Make sure that you know the worldview of those to whom you run for advice.

Third, crowdsource parenting is dangerous because your kids do not deserve to be exploited. The whole world does not need to know that Judy is wetting the bed or throwing tantrums, or getting into trouble at school. You should love your kids enough to seek wise counsel on how to parent them, but you should also love them enough to do it as discreetly as possible. Once you put it online, it is there forever. Remember, the battle is not you against your kids. It is you and your kids against a sinful world that would rob them of their joy and keep them separated from God forever.

Finally, crowdsource parenting should be avoided

because you need to be reminded that the world does not revolve around you. Egos get padded when people comment on status updates. Using your family problems as an avenue to rack up hits on your blog, increase Instagram likes, or collect Facebook comments is narcissistic and inappropriate. It feeds your pride and starves your soul.

I determined early in parenting to get permission from my elementary-aged kids before posting anything about them online or mentioning them in a sermon. The reasons vary for each child. For instance, at six and seven, my kids began to grasp the gravity of social media. One of my kids understood quickly that *EVERYONE* can see what is posted online and didn't want me to post because they might get embarrassed. Another child understood that *EVERYONE* could see what is posted online and really wanted to gain the online notoriety of being widely known. In either case, social media was not healthy for any of my kids and was definitely not beneficial for my parenting. I'm not against all crowdsourcing, but I'm utterly convinced that the advice I receive from those who know me best and share my worldview will trump the advice I would get from hundreds of Facebook comments. I may never be Facebook famous, but that shouldn't be my goal anyway. If I ever design a cooler, I'll look for advice and funding online, but for my kids, I'll stick with God's word and his people to help me raise them up right.

A Team Approach Toward Parenting

But if crowdsourcing is wrong, then what does a team approach look like, and how can it help us to find victory in spiritual warfare? The team approach to parenting must include your spouse, your extended family, your church family, AND your kids. For married couples, a team approach means working together and presenting a united front. Being a part of a team as a young man was always one of my greatest joys. On my high school football team, loyalty was taught above all else—you take care of each other. As parents, husband and wife must make the decision to be on the same team raising their kids. Children are born sinful, so they will often interact with their parents in sinful ways, and they will divide and conquer if they can. Christian parents must be absolutely convinced of the biblical pattern of marriage and family. Husbands are to love their wives as Christ loved his church, wives are to serve and submit to their husbands, and children are to honor their parents. Ultimately, the team approach to parenting looks biblical. It is a mom and dad working together to raise their children.

The greatest gift parents will give to their children is a healthy and happy family. Healthy families are those made up of parents who prioritize their commitment to each other over their kids. God's design for marriage has always prioritized the marriage relationship. The husband and wife become "one flesh" through the marriage covenant, but there is a temptation to allow parenting to create a division in the "one flesh" union. Moms and dads should affirm their commitment to each other in front of their children regularly. Dance in the kitchen, kiss in the dining room, discuss (and agree on) discipline in private conversations.

The primary goal of parenting is not to raise happy children, but godly adults. In Deuteronomy 6, one of the great scriptural passages on parenting, Moses commanded the Israelites, "The Lord our God, the Lord is one. You shall love the Lord your God with all your heart and with all your soul and with all your might." Regarding these words, they are then commanded,

> *You shall teach them diligently to your children and shall talk of them when you sit in your house, and when you walk by the way, and when you lie down, and when you rise. You shall bind them as a sign on your hand, and they shall be as frontlets between your eyes. You shall write them on the doorposts of your house and on your gates.[6]*

The primary responsibility of parents is to teach their children to love the Lord, but that responsibility does not eclipse the responsibility to model Christ to the world through a committed marriage relationship.

---

[6] Deuteronomy 6:4-9

In Ephesians 5:32, Paul shows that the union between husband and wife is an important witness of Christ to the world.

> *"This mystery is profound, and I am saying that it refers to Christ and the church."*

Husband and wife must work with one mind in parenting because their unity and marital health serve as a model of Christ's relationship with his church to their children as much as it does to the world outside of their family. The dedication of husband to wife and wife to husband creates safety and stability within the family structure that limits Satan's activities and provides a sense of safety and security for children. Contrary to what some may believe, in making the spousal commitment primary in the marriage, parents do not neglect their children. Instead, they provide an environment that encourages healthy physical, emotional, and spiritual growth among children.

There is Strength in Numbers

A team is nothing if they are not united. To make parenting a team sport, you must make the team a priority in your life. As mentioned above, there are two primary teams that are important for parenting and for creating a Christian family. The first team is your family. As parents, that means, first and foremost, each other. If you are going to work together in raising your kids, then you must spend time together. You must be committed to being together and sacrificing individual time and hobbies for the purpose of building a family that honors Christ. A healthy marriage is one where husband and wife interact with interdependence, relishing time together, and depending upon one another. Strong couples make time to be together and to grow together in Christ by exploring spiritual terrain as a couple. Christ must be cherished in the marital union if that love for Christ is to be passed to the next generation.

> Raising kids that honor Christ is best accomplished within a family that honors Christ and prioritizes commitment to Christ's church.

Raising kids that honor Christ is best accomplished within a family that honors Christ and prioritizes commitment to Christ's church. It is easy to find excuses to neglect the church and regular church attendance. Life is busy. There are sports and hobbies even on Sundays that draw people away from the church. For others, because life is so busy Monday through Saturday, some families find church commitment a struggle because Sunday is the only day that is not consumed with other responsibilities. Despite multitudes of excuses, parents accomplish at least two things by committing to church membership and regular attendance. First, commitment to a local church signifies to your children that you place a high priority on your commitment to Christ. If the old adage, "more is caught than taught," is true, then telling our children we love Jesus does not impact them nearly as much unless they see that love in action. Committing to regular church attendance shows children that commitment to Christ is palpable rather than ethereal. Regular church attendance says, "I love Jesus, and I want to be with Jesus and his people."

> Commitment to a local church shows your children that you take Jesus's words seriously. The church is not a creation of man; it is the creation of Christ.

Of course, commitment to a local church also shows your children that you take Jesus's words seriously. The church is not a creation of man; it is the creation of Christ.[7] The Bible says that the church is the bride of Christ.[8] Committing to the church is committing to the bride of Christ. Solidifying and cherishing this relationship with a local church is a valuable and effective weapon in spiritual warfare.

Regular attendance at your local church provides you with a large family to support the spiritual formation of your children. I learned this valuable lesson through experience with our church family when our oldest daughter broke her leg. Our then 5-year-old daughter hurt her leg one Saturday, and an X-ray the next day

---

[7] Matthew 16:18
[8] Ephesians 5:25-27

revealed that her femur was broken. Her leg was splinted, and she was miserable. Her attitude was terrible, and her normally bubbly personality was nearly non-existent. Angela and I briefly contemplated not taking her to church for our services on Sunday night because it was going to be difficult for us, and because she was so miserable (of course, we were miserable too).

We soon discovered that it would have been a disservice to Aubrey to keep her away from her church family during a time of great stress and trial in her young life. Our temptation was to retreat into our comfortable home and stable family. That temptation would have resulted in movie time with Mom for Aubrey, but it would also have meant that Aubrey would not have experienced the love of her church family. We left home with a nervous, anxious, and sad little girl. At church, we put Aubrey in a red wagon and pulled her through the halls of our church building. Our church family enveloped her with kind words, hugs, smiles, and even small gifts. Later that night, Aubrey left the church excited and encouraged. Because of her church family, her little red wagon had been transformed from her cart of suffering into her little chariot of joy.

Many people assume that my commitment to regular church attendance is based primarily upon the fact that I'm a pastor—more of a "well, of course you think it's important," rather than an understanding of why regular church attendance matters. The reality is that church attendance *must* matter to Christian families *because* it matters to God. You should gather for encouragement,[9] and the book of Hebrews warns you not to forsake these gatherings. There are times when church attendance isn't convenient or doesn't seem beneficial, but it is especially during those times that church attendance is crucial. It is during those times of struggle, and even heartache, that God's church is powerful in helping you overcome spiritual struggles.

The warning to the Hebrews was that temptations and trials from the world would seek to drive God's people away from regularly meeting together with their church family. The exhortation to the Hebrews, however, was that gathering together for fellowship and worship was worth the cost. God created people as relational beings. You need your church. Yes, if the church is doing its job, then the people of the church are caring for those in need during times outside of the normal meetings, but unless you are making yourself available during normal gathering times, the church is often unaware of your struggle or trial. This is especially true in parenting. You need your church to help you raise your children well.

> Faithful commitment to a church provides help for raising your children well.

Healthy churches are filled with people from different walks of life and various generations. Their varied

---
[9] Hebrews 10:25

experiences and spiritual insights enable them to speak into your life and your current struggle. Faithful church attendance helps you to raise your children by giving you access to parents who have already raised their children into adulthood. These believers can serve as guides to young parents trying to maneuver children through adolescence. Regular church attendance gives your children regular access to other godly adults who can reinforce the lessons you are teaching your kids at home.

Regular church attendance is not only for the kids. Adults need their church family, too. Satan seeks to separate you from your church family because his desire is to steal, kill, and destroy,[10] and that is a much easier task with a solitary sheep than with those who are gathered together under the shepherd's protection. When do you need to gather with your church the most?

You need the church the most when you desire it the least and when you have the least time for it. You need encouragement and exhortation that comes from engagement with God's people and God's word. Are you in sin?

> You need the church the most when you desire it the least and when you have the least time for it.

Gather with your church family so that you may hear words of correction.[11] Are you under attack? Gather

---
[10] John 10:10
[11] 2 Timothy 4:2

for protection. Are you weak, sick, or hurting? Gather so that the church can pray for you.[12]

Don't hide. When life gets hard, there is a temptation to retreat into your shell and hide from the world, and even from your church family. During difficult seasons of life, I continue to be grateful for what a broken leg taught me about the importance of church attendance. Are you worried that if you attend church, your kid might embarrass you? It is OK. Your church is a safe place—safe for you and your kids. Go there to find others who know your pain and struggle. Let someone else help you for a while.

When our kids are sick and have to miss church, they ask us constantly when they will be able to return to church. Why? Because it is there that they feel most at home, around their extended spiritual family who regularly take it upon themselves to encourage and exhort them toward physical and spiritual healing. A healthy church family is a wonderful picture of God's family, behaving like Christ, binding up the broken and bandaging the wounded. Satan's goal is to separate you, but the spirit of Christ is one of unity.[13]

> The church is a place of healing, but your church family can only care for you when they can get to you.

What did a broken leg teach us? We learned that the church

---

[12] James 5:14
[13] Ephesians 4:2-3

is a place of healing, but your church family can only care for you when they can get to you. There is encouragement in the fellowship of your brothers and sisters in Christ. So go gather with your church. You need them, and they need you. Parenting is a team sport, and your church family is an important part of the team.

PRACTICAL APPLICATION

We Bought a Fire Pit

The team aspect of parenting should remind us of the importance of spending time together. ***The days are long, but the years are short*** is a wise saying that was spoken to Angela and me when our kids were younger. When our oldest son started his senior year of high school, I was reminded again of that sage wisdom. Some days as a parent seem to last a month. And yet, as holidays roll around or birthdays are celebrated, we all find ourselves sounding more and more like our parents: "They sure do grow up fast."

Your days are numbered with your kids. From birth to

eighteen (when we sort of hope they will begin to leave the nest), you have about 936 weekends. 936 Saturdays. 936 Sundays. Actually, you don't even have all of those. Of the 936 Saturdays that your kids will spend on this earth during their first 18 years, many of them will be spent away from you. You may travel, or they might go to a friend's house or visit with grandparents.

Your 936 gets cut down to 836 or 736. If you happen to be a family separated by divorce, you may only have your kids half of those days. Maybe your number is 400 or 425.

Depressed yet?

I hope not. I'm not writing to depress anyone, just to remind you that the days may be long, but the years are short. Because the years are short, it is imperative that you invest all you can into the years that you have with your kids.

In our family, one of our efforts at investment is to get away from screens regularly and spend time enjoying each other. That means we love walks and sports. It also means that we must double down on entertainment ideas that keep us away from the television.

That's why we bought a fire pit.

Angela and I wanted to create an excuse to be outside together. But we are also realistic. Sometimes, our kids find us boring, and getting them away from screens can be a fight.

Kids don't find fire boring.

They love everything about fire. They love building fires, poking fires, and even putting out fires. Kids love s'mores and hot dogs over an open flame. Give them the opportunity, and your kids may even find joy and satisfaction in splitting wood and adding it to the fire.

We bought a fire pit because we believe in family, and we believe it is our job to instill in our kids a love for Jesus and each other.

Consider the words of Paul in 2 Timothy 3:14-15:

> *But as for you, continue in what you have learned and have firmly believed, knowing from whom you learned it and how from childhood you have been acquainted with the sacred writings, which are able to make you wise for salvation through faith in Christ Jesus.*

We bought a fire pit because we believe that discipleship should happen in the normal course of everyday life. We believe that the gospel needs to be taught in childhood. We believe that kids learn dominion as they cut and split wood. We believe that fellowship around an open fire opens the door for intentional dialogue.

We have heard our kids open up about their joys, their fears, and their failures when their attention is focused on dancing flames.

We believe that Saturday nights are great times to slow down and prepare our hearts for Sunday worship.

PRACTICAL APPLICATION

We believe that the warm glow of a roaring fire is often healthier than the cold blue radiance of a screen.

For all of these reasons and more, we bought a fire pit. We went all in and bought a really nice fire pit that should last long enough for our grandkids to enjoy. We spent almost as much money on our fire pit as we did on our TV.

But should you spend all that money on a fire pit?

Not necessarily. You can dig a fire pit with a shovel. You can build a fire in a cut-off oil drum or create a fire-ring with rocks or bricks.

You might not even need a fire pit. But you'd better invest in your kids. You'd better invest in your family. You might not choose a fire pit, but you need to find ways to teach your kids to be good stewards of technology. Fire pits, swimming pools, or lazy afternoons by the ocean, are great ways to remind your children that many of life's greatest joys do not come from screens. Walks in the woods and bike rides through your community teach your kids to pay attention to their surroundings and often teach them to navigate challenges.

If you aren't careful, the digital devices in your life and in the lives of your children will not serve to enhance those 936 Saturdays. Instead, the digital devices will rob you of Saturdays. You will discover that pings, dings, updates, and messages from the world of digital space interfere with your face-to-face encounters with your family.

Remember, you have 936 Saturdays. Unless you are reading this today and you have a 9-year-old, in which case you have half that many. Time is fleeting. You have opportunities and responsibilities, but you don't have forever. When you teach your children to unplug and steward their digital technology well, you teach them to live in the world around them. You teach them to value real-life relationships and to enjoy the beauty of the world God created.

Consider the ways you might steward your own devices to maximize time with your family. You might use the calendar feature on your phone to add a family night to the shared family calendar so that everyone can see the specific times that are set aside for family time. You might use your messaging app to remind everyone that a particular Saturday is reserved. You can Google "campfire activities" for ideas about how to spend your time around the fire pit. You might even open your Notes app and jot down a grocery list or a short family devotion, or a list of conversation starters for the big night. You can use your phone to create a music playlist.

Technology isn't bad. Your phone is not evil. It can even be helpful. Everything you need for your big fire-pit night might get planned out and saved on your phone.

Just as your phone can be your best friend in planning your big night, phones can also be the greatest enemy to enjoying your big night. The same phone that helped you to get ready can be the distraction that destroys your fire pit adventure. Instead of playing games together, your kids are playing games alone. Instead of enjoying your family, you are scrolling through Instagram looking at someone else's family photos. Rather than playing music over the Bluetooth speaker, your daughter has her earbuds in, ignoring everyone else.

In the 21st Century, teaching kids the discipline of digital stewardship is a requirement for parents. Digital devices have become a necessary part of daily life. As a parent, it is your responsibility to teach your kids how to keep digital things in their proper place and time. How will you teach them? Remember Deuteronomy 4:7: "when you sit in your house, and when you walk by the way, and when you lie down, and when you rise. "

The greatest lessons you will teach your children about the discipline of digital stewardship will come from *your* example. Kids are not only watching to see if you are disciplined in your use of technology; they are watching to see if you are a person of integrity in the rules you give or follow. If you lie about their age so they can sign up to social media services, they are learning that honesty is only important when it is convenient.

Your children are watching you, and they are slowly becoming you. Do you believe that your digital devices take up an appropriate amount of time and attention in your life? Do you exercise intentional discipline over your digital devices?

When your kids see you making analog priorities, they will understand the value that exists outside of the digital world. In our family, a fire pit has helped us to prioritize the analog over the digital. Consider these practical steps to teach your children digital stewardship.

Require permission to watch TV or use digital devices.

This may seem like over-parenting at first, but the idea is to create a culture in your home where digital is not the default. Like other things in your home, digital devices are tools. Other tools in your home are turned "off" unless they are needed. You don't leave your hairdryer on all the time just to create background noise or to heat your bathroom. In analog families, the default for digital devices is off. Bored kids are encouraged to play games, go outside, or enjoy the experience of boredom.

It is OK to be bored.

In fact, boredom can often lead to creativity. But if you allow all of your child's bored moments to be filled with digital junk food, they will never experience that creative explosion. Don't use your TV for background noise. Don't use your phone or other screens as a babysitter. Require your kids to get permission to use their digital devices.

Do not allow phones at the table.

For the sake of this book, we are assuming that you make family mealtime a regular priority. When you sit down at the table, make sure that phones go somewhere else. And yes, that includes your phone. The family should receive undivided attention around the table. Be present physically, emotionally, and mentally.

> Make family mealtime a regular priority.

Kids pick up on your subtle cues. When you are staring at your phone, they know that you aren't paying them any attention. They are also learning from you. If you ignore them at mealtimes, don't be surprised if they pay you the same honor.

Wait to give your kids a mobile phone.

What is the best age? You must be the judge for the exact age in your home, but it is hard to conceive of a good reason for an elementary school kid to have a phone of their own. Remember,

> You don't give chainsaws to 8-year-olds. Don't give them a phone either.

digital devices are tools. Do not give your kid a tool that could harm them before they can manage it. You don't give chainsaws to 8-year-olds. Don't give them a phone either.

Learn to use parental controls.

It is okay if you don't know how to set up parental controls on your digital devices or your home internet router. It is not okay if you put your kids at risk by refusing to learn how to manage parental controls.

When the time came to buy phones for our two oldest kids, they got our old iPhones. There were cheaper options out there, but I am familiar with the Apple ecosystem. I know how they work. I know how to set up parental controls without needing to learn a different operating system. As a result, we decided it was worth spending a little more money to give us the peace of mind.

Parental controls on your kids' devices should be a requirement. It doesn't matter if they like it. It doesn't matter what their friends do. Make sure your kids are protected from adult websites. Even better, block the web-browsing app from your kids' phones until they are a little older.

Just say no to social media.

Social media can be fun. But, for kids under 16, the danger is far too great to ignore. Facebook's and Instagram's own internal studies determined that Instagram's platform made "body image issues worse for one in three teen girls."[1] The same report indicates that up to 13% of suicidal teens in the UK point to Instagram as the source for their initial suicidal impulses.

Decide to avoid social media apps and websites as long as possible. Like other digital content and devices, social media is not necessarily evil in and of itself. There is good to be found there. But your kids have to be taught how to manage social media. They will learn that from you as they see you managing social media. Don't expect them to learn healthy habits of social media management by giving them unfettered access to social media platforms at age 11.

What does all of this mean? Your kids are watching you. And by your example, they are learning how to be disciplined in their digital technology.

> Your kids are watching you. And by your example, they are learning how to be disciplined in their digital technology.

I don't like roasted marshmallows. But I love time with my kids that is uninterrupted

---

[1] www.theverge.com/2021/9/15/22675130/facebook-instagram-teens-mental-health-damage-internal-research.

by television and video games. I love burning paper plates instead of washing dishes. And I love that, after the kids go to bed, sometimes I get to sneak a few minutes alone by the fire with my wife—the woman God gave to me and our children.

We bought a fire pit because we wanted an excuse to spend time together and build memories as a family.

Consider these ideas or create your own list:
- bike rides
- nature walks
- hunting trips
- hikes
- family read-alouds
- camp outs (outside or in the family room)
- ice cream on the front porch
- rucking
- tech-free coffee dates
- dinner at your favorite restaurant
- fishing

What excuses are you creating to spend time with your family?

CHAPTER FIVE

Fighting for Intimacy

Each man should have his own wife, and each woman her own husband. The husband should give to his wife her conjugal rights, and likewise the wife to her husband. For the wife does not have authority over her own body, but the husband does. Likewise, the husband does not have authority over his own body, but the wife does.

1 Corinthians 7:3-4

If you are reading this and do not have kids, you

FIGHTING ~~WITH~~ *FOR* YOUR FAMILY

probably do not appreciate the fact that this chapter follows a chapter on parenting. If you have kids, then you understand well that among all the challenges to maintaining intimacy in your marriage, children are probably the greatest. Before kids come along, intimacy can be spontaneous. On the spur of the moment, you can run out for a nice dinner or light some candles and turn the kitchen into a 5-star restaurant for two. You can cuddle on the couch or make out in the laundry room. You don't even need locks on bedroom doors.

> The battle to maintain intimacy takes the cunning of a spy, the fortitude of a Navy SEAL, the careful scheduling of a fortune 500 secretary, and the locks of Fort Knox.

But when kids come along, the battle to maintain intimacy takes the cunning of a spy, the fortitude of a Navy SEAL, the careful scheduling of a Fortune 500 secretary, and the locks of Fort Knox. Even then, trips can be cancelled because of stomach viruses, dates can be cut short by emergency room visits, and cuddling on the couch elicits groans and vomit sounds from the little intimacy police guarding your house. Think I'm exaggerating? We have friends who took careful precautions to have some intimate time after their kids were asleep. Imagine their surprise when, in the darkness of their bedroom, a kid slid from under the bed and shouted, "SURPRISE!" Needless to say, their plans were altered as they screamed, "Get out of here and DO NOT TURN ON THE LIGHT!"

Maintaining intimacy is a challenge, but kids are not the only obstacle. Life gets in the way. Jobs are stressful, family members have needs, our church responsibilities can wear us out, and sometimes we are just tired. Regardless of the challenge, intimacy is a necessary ingredient in any Christian family that hopes to honor Christ and experience victory in spiritual warfare. As we saw in chapter two, Paul identifies healthy sexual relations as a necessary component of spiritual warfare. Let's look at 1 Corinthians 7:1-7 so that we can see the context:

> *Now concerning the matters about which you wrote: "It is good for a man not to have sexual relations with a woman." But because of the temptation to sexual immorality, each man should have his own wife and each woman her own husband. The husband should give to his wife her conjugal rights, and likewise the wife to her husband. For the wife does not have authority over her own body, but the husband does. Likewise the husband does not have authority over his own body, but the wife does. Do not deprive one another, except perhaps by agreement for a limited time, that you may devote yourselves to prayer; but then come together again, so that*

Satan may not tempt you because of your lack of self-control.

> A healthy sexual relationship with your spouse is a necessary component of spiritual warfare.

The teaching is clear. Husbands and wives are to deny Satan a foothold in their marriage by enjoying a healthy sex life. A healthy sex life is a natural and important component of any resilient marriage, but intimacy does not begin and end with sex. In fact, a healthy sex life is more than the sexual act. A healthy sex life is an important part of a marriage that has a healthy view of sex and a healthy approach to intimacy. Intimacy doesn't just happen. You have to fight for intimacy in your marriage.

Recognize the Need for Intimacy

Naked and not ashamed. That is the description given of Adam and Eve shortly after Eve's introduction. In South Carolina, we do not say naked (that's a medical term); they were "nekkid." It wasn't just that they weren't wearing clothes. They were completely exposed—and yet they were not ashamed. Why?

They had nothing to be ashamed of. There was no sin, and there were no failures or shortcomings. Some have suggested that these two human creations were magnificently beautiful and would have had no physical defects to make them ashamed. That may be true, but the Bible doesn't tell us that. It only tells us that after God created them, he noted that they were "good."

They could be naked and not ashamed because there was no sinful past. They didn't perceive themselves as being judged because they themselves were not judgmental. No one had ever pointed out their big legs, or small chest, or long nose. They had never used their bodies to get the attention of another, nor had they ever experienced the shame of having their bodies abused or exploited by someone else.

After sin entered the world, Adam and Eve were no longer unashamed. They suddenly felt their nakedness. They were exposed, and they were guilty. They were ashamed—not primarily because someone had exploited them. They were ashamed because they were guilty.

Many of you reading this may struggle with shame, not because of what has been done to you, but because of what you have done. You rightly understand that you are a sinner, and intimacy is terrifying. Being exposed in front of another is scary because they may discover the "you" that you have so carefully hidden. So, just like Adam and Eve, you patch together coverings of leaves, you hide in the bushes, you avoid intimacy at all costs. Sure, you go through the motions of marriage. You may even have regular sex, but you keep your guard up.

Modern psychologists influenced by Eastern religious thought would have us believe that guilt is a false emotion we must ignore. We are not truly guilty, they say. Guilt is only a feeling that we have been programmed to feel. Overcoming feelings of guilt is about coming to terms with the person you are and recognizing that who you are is OK. But the biblical worldview is different. According to the Bible, you *are* guilty. The barrier to intimacy in your marriage is not that you have assigned yourself a false sense of guilt. You are guilty, and only Christ can take away your guilt. You are afraid of intimacy because you have not trusted Christ to cover your sin and make you clean and whole.

For as many as there are who feel ashamed because of the sin in their own past, there are others who feel shame because of sins committed against them. Your shame may not be rooted only in your actions, but in pain, shame, and abuse from your past. For those who have experienced abuse, neglect, or exploitation, intimacy is shame-inducing and often terrifying. But you do not have to live in fear or shame of what has been done to you. Jesus died to set you free from the sins you have committed, but also to deliver you from the pain of sin committed against you. You do not have to live in captivity to the pain of your past. Jesus died to set you free. Your freedom in Christ means eternal life, but it can also mean freedom in this life to experience real intimacy with the spouse God has given you, despite the pain of your past. Jesus

> You do not have to live in captivity to the pain of your past. Jesus died to set you free.

loves you and wants to heal your hurts and give you an opportunity to be "naked and not ashamed" with your spouse.

The first step in fighting for intimacy with your husband or wife is to recognize the need that you have for intimacy. Intimacy is more than a good idea—it is a human need. Just as you need food and air and shelter, you need intimate relationships with others. Because you need intimacy, anything that keeps you from experiencing intimacy with your spouse needs to be healed by Jesus's love. You need non-romantic friendships as well, but for the sake of this book, we are focusing on the need you have for intimacy in your marriage. When God designed marriage, he created it as a one-flesh union. But this one-flesh union is much more than what the Spice Girls envisioned in the 90s when they sang, *When Two Become One*. Sex is great, but marriage is not about sex; it is about intimacy, and sex is only one aspect of intimacy in marriage. You can live without sex. Sex consummates and solidifies a marriage, but sex is not the foundation for intimacy. A good sex life is the reward for intimacy.

Understand the Concept of Intimacy

Once you have established and understood that intimacy is necessary in your marriage, you must understand what intimacy is. As we pointed out earlier, the book of Genesis describes intimacy as "naked and not ashamed." In Genesis 2:24, we learn, "Therefore a man shall leave his father and his mother and hold fast to his wife and they shall become one flesh." Intimacy is rooted in the one-flesh union of husband and wife, where each person is changed.

Intimacy is the living out of the one-flesh union of husband and wife. As mentioned above, sex is a component of marital intimacy, but it is only one component, and, in many ways, it is the reward for intimacy. Lasting intimacy is not only flesh-to-flesh in the dark; it is face-to-face in the light. Intimacy involves listening and doing. An intimate relationship is one where the partners know one another completely. In fact, marital intimacy involves the kind of complete knowledge that can often result in deeper love *because* of imperfections or past pain.

Understanding marital intimacy necessitates a robust understanding of intimacy. Marital intimacy is one form of intimacy, but it is not the only kind of intimacy. People can be said to have an intimate relationship with God. Strong friendships can be intimate without being sexual in nature. Like other forms of intimacy, marital intimacy must be built on shared experiences and mutual trust. Friendships are forged over time. Even our relationship with God grows deeper—more intimate—as we experience him more through worship and his Word. So, too, intimacy in marriage is forged as couples spend purposeful time together.

Biblical intimacy in marriage is possible, not because spouses are perfect, but because they are committed to covenant love. From the beginning, marriage was designed to be a picture to the world of the covenant between Christ and his church.[1] John Piper explains,

> "The very essence of this new covenant is that Christ passes over the sins of his bride. His bride is free from shame, not because she is perfect, but because she has no fear that her lover will condemn her or shame her because of her sin."[2]

Thus, the concept of intimacy in marriage is rooted in the love that Christ has for his bride, the church. Husbands and wives should practice the same kind of selfless love toward one another—a love that covers sin and shame. This kind of love results in liberty among lovers, the kind of intimate liberty that enables spouses to know one another and be fully known.

This kind of intimacy requires intentionality. Life-giving, sin-covering love is built upon a foundation of deliberate dating and purposeful romance. The kind of love that Christ has for his church is self-sacrificing. It is important to really understand Jesus's sacrifice and how it can deepen marital intimacy.

---
[1] Ephesians 5:31-32
[2] Piper, John. *This Momentary Marriage*. Crossway, 2009. p.33-34.

Jesus did not die for the church because of all the church would do or had done for him. Jesus died for the church because of the church's sin. Jesus died to reconcile the church to himself. Jesus died so that the church could find intimacy with him.

Husbands and wives are called to love one another with a Christ-like love. That love is the kind of love that sacrifices for the sake of intimacy. Christ-like love is the kind of love that sees the sin and shame of the past in our spouses and wraps them in covenantal love anyway.

Christ-like love in marriage, which leads to intimacy, is also the kind of love that seeks to forgive as Christ forgives. The Psalmist wrote of the Lord this way, "For as high as the heavens are above the earth, so great is his steadfast love toward those who fear him; as far as the east is from the west, so far does he remove our transgressions from us."[3] Isaiah wrote of the Lord, "I, I am he who blots out your transgressions for my own sake, and I will not remember your sins."[4] Intimacy in marriage is built by spouses who know the past but choose to forgive and forget it. Intimacy in marriage is often destroyed by spouses who know the past and choose to use it as a tool for leverage or a bludgeoning weapon in a disagreement.

If you can't get past the sexual sin of your wife's past,

---
[3] Psalm 103:11-12
[4] Isaiah 43:25

that is not her fault; it is yours. Jesus has forgiven. If you hold a grudge against your husband's high school girlfriend, that is not his fault; it is yours. Jesus knows your sin and chooses to forgive you and love you anyway. The goal of intimacy is to know the gory details and to love anyway. That kind of love is a choice and a decision. That kind of love is not always easy, but it is possible. That kind of love takes time, energy, and effort.

Make a Plan for Intimacy

When marriage progresses into parenthood and increased responsibilities, freedom can seem to fall by the wayside. When you lose some of that initial freedom, planning becomes an important part of intimacy. As you plan, you need to plan for the face-to-face, in-the-light kind of intimacy and the flesh-to-flesh, in-the-dark kind of intimacy. While it is true that intimacy is built on face-to-face time in the light, couples must not neglect to plan for the kinds of intimacy that take place primarily in the dark.

> The goal of intimacy is to know the gory details and to love anyway.

Planning for intimacy does not seem very romantic. In fact, when this part of marriage counseling comes up, ladies often roll their eyes. The very idea of planning dates in advance, or, gasp, planning sex in advance, seems to lack the spontaneity that Hollywood has programmed us to expect in romance. Hollywood, however, is a fairy tale. In fact, based on the revelations about the sex culture in Hollywood following the Harvey Weinstein discoveries and the #MeToo movement, it is a fairy tale that even Hollywood doesn't reflect.

Intimacy and romance in real life require work and planning. Life is busy, and the things that matter get planned. You make it to your doctor's appointments and sports games because they are on your calendar. They matter, so they get scheduled and then planned around. Nothing in your life outside of your relationship with Christ should matter more than your spouse. Therefore, time with your spouse should be scheduled on your calendar. It should get planned and planned around.

> Life is busy, and the things that matter get planned.

Remember that planning for intimacy doesn't have to be elaborate (though it can be occasionally), and it is not only sexual intimacy that deserves careful thought and planning. Through the years, Angela and I have discovered that when the kids are in school, lunch dates work well for us. Since we have four kids, finding babysitters can be a challenge, so we make the most of our situation. But, even then, we must plan ahead. Notice, I said, "we." Planning to grow in intimacy should be a joint effort. Sit down with a calendar and make a plan that works for each of you. Talk about your shared expectations. Some couples find plenty of time to be together after the kids go to bed, while others need much more time. Perhaps you have easy access to babysitters, and you can arrange a date night every other weekend. Find out what works best for each situation.

Consider planning your sexual intimacy as well. Many couples benefit from planning regular times to have sex. Planning your sex life forces you to verbalize expectations that often go unspoken and, when they do, result in frustration and argument. Often, marital problems and problems with intimacy are chalked up to "communication problems." The problem is not the lack of communication. The reason that your problems do not get dealt with is actually the lack of *honest* communication. When it comes to sex, conversations can be awkward and uncomfortable, but if you talk about it, you might find that sex doesn't have to be a point of contention in your marriage.

When you sit down with your spouse to plan your sex life, you will quickly discover where your expectations about sex differ (your "sexpectations"). One of you might think that healthy couples should have sex three times per week. The other may believe that healthy couples have sex three times per month. If you differ that widely on expectations about sex, it is safe to assume your sex life has probably been a point of regular strife.

Couples find it difficult to grow in sexual intimacy when the bedroom is a place of regular conflict. But you can overcome much of the conflict in your bedroom through honest communication. Making a plan about your sex life requires you to communicate clearly. By talking about your sex life and making plans to make it healthy, your face-to-face intimacy can intersect with flesh-on-flesh intimacy. Planning makes it possible for a spouse with a lower sex drive to prepare ahead. For a spouse with a higher sex drive, planning gives him or her something to look forward to.

There are some rare couples who have matching sex drives and seem to have no need to plan out their sex life. That probably isn't you. Most couples could benefit by talking about sexual expectations. At the end of the day, you have to figure out what works for you. Maybe you need to organize your sex life with Google Calendar. Then again, maybe your marriage can be happy if sex happens every Friday night. Regardless, if you are going to fight for success in your marriage, healthy sexual intimacy will be a key component, and it will be most healthy if you have open conversations with one another about how to fulfill each other's needs. Paul was clear when he wrote that each partner in marriage should elevate the needs of the other ahead of their own sexual desires.[5] If you work diligently to outdo one another in showing love in and out of the

---
[5] 1 Corinthians 7:1-7

bedroom, you will find that intimacy is not a distant fantasy, but a glorious reality in your marriage.

Deny Satan a Foothold

You have to fight for intimacy in your marriage because the fight for intimacy is, in fact, the fight for your marriage. When you maintain healthy intimacy in your marriage, you deny Satan a foothold. If your spouse is satisfied at home, they are less likely to be tempted to look for satisfaction elsewhere and are much more immune to attacks from the devil on this front. Your bedroom is a place of warfare, but not with each other. You are battling for your marriage, and it is a fight that is worth your time, even if it requires the planning of a Fortune 500 assistant and the cunning of a CIA agent.

> Your bedroom is a place of warfare, but not with each other.

PRACTICAL APPLICATION

Guarding Intimacy

"I have made a covenant with my eyes; how then could I gaze at a virgin?

Job 31:1

Job 31 is titled, "Job's Final Appeal." It is Job's last defense of his holiness, and he begins his defense with his eyes. Holiness for Job does not begin with his sexual activity. It does not begin with his financial dealings. Holiness begins where he directs his eyes.

As you consider what it looks like in your marriage

to fight for intimacy, begin with your own eyes. We live in a world that is constantly striving to steal our attention, and nothing sells faster or easier than sex. At the same time, nothing can destroy intimacy in your marriage faster than allowing extra-marital sexual activity to enter your life. But, extramarital sexual activity is more than having sex with someone else. Jesus warned that to look at another with lustful intent was to commit adultery in your heart.[1]

With that in mind, certain things should always be out of bounds for followers of Christ, beginning with your eyes. Pornography is wrong. When you choose to look at other people engaged in sexual activities for your own sexual satisfaction, you do great damage to the bonds of intimacy in your own life. Avoiding pornography is not easy because it is almost everywhere in our culture today, but fighting for purity is a necessity in the Christian life. It is also important to remember that pornography is more than trashy photos or movies.

The word pornography comes from a Greek word, *porneia,* which has a wide range of meanings, including fornication, sexual immorality, or illicit sexual relations. According to Blue Letter Bible.[2] Porneia encompasses various forms of sexual activity outside of what is

---
[1] Matthew 5:28
[2] www.blueletterbible.com

considered permissible. Sexual sin, therefore, includes things like romance novels and risque text messages. Unfortunately, it has become somewhat acceptable in some circles for even Christians to read sleazy romance novels, but just as sexually explicit photos damage intimacy within marriage, so too do romance novels and films or TV shows that involve explicit sexual activity.

Job made a covenant with his eyes, and so should believers today. Covenant to keep your eyes focused on your spouse for sexual satisfaction. And, covenant to keep your eyes from idolatry as well. The wandering eye of a husband toward other women for satisfaction constitutes a form of infidelity. The wandering eye of anyone toward an idol for satisfaction instead of toward the Lord constitutes infidelity toward the Lord.

> Covenant to keep your eyes focused on your spouse for sexual satisfaction.

Choose to make a covenant with your eyes—have eyes only for the God who created you and the spouse to whom he has given you. If you will guard your eyes, intimacy in other areas is easier to protect and to cultivate.

CHAPTER SIX

Fighting for Holiness

Husbands, love your wives, as Christ loved the church and gave himself up for her, that he might sanctify her, having cleansed her by the washing of water with the word, so that he might present the church to himself in splendor, without spot or wrinkle or any such thing, that she might be holy and without blemish. In the same way, husbands should love their wives as their own bodies.

Ephesians 5:25-28

The story goes that this particular husband had a long and celebrated military career, including work with the Joint Chiefs of Staff. During a visit to his wife's hometown, he and his wife stopped at a gas station, and the attendant recognized the general's wife. She climbed out of the car, and they laughed and reminisced about old times as the general stood by watching. Pulling out of the station, the general commented to his wife, "See, if you hadn't met me, you might have married him. You should thank me for the life I've saved you from." His wife quickly corrected him. "No, honey, if I had married him, he'd be the general and you'd be pumping gas."

One of our responsibilities and opportunities in marriage is to build up our spouse and to see them become more holy. A wife should be a better woman because of the man she marries; a husband should be a better man because of the woman he marries. This is common sense. Behind every good man is a good woman, but I can assure you that most good women also have the support of a good man.

The picture of the ideal woman is found in Proverbs 31. As mentioned in Chapter 1, the Proverbs 31 woman was both enterprising and godly. She worked outside the home and labored to serve her family well. She was respected and honored. Women want to be the Proverbs 31 woman, and men want to be married to her. She appears to have had everything going for her.

One of her greatest attributes is that she made much of her husband and children, and her love toward her household gave her family great renown. Her husband was known in the gates. He was a ruler and was respected by his peers; no doubt, the strong character of his wife was an asset to his civic responsibilities.

Just like the woman of Proverbs 31, wives of today should work to see their husbands thrive. But we should also note that the Proverbs 31 wife had a Proverbs 31 husband. It was her husband who spoke this Proverb in her honor or in her memory. Through his words, we learn something about the man who supported this amazing woman.

• He counted her as more precious than jewels (10).

• He trusted his wife completely, which was not a common practice in the Ancient Near East (11).

• He recognized her enterprising nature and trusted that she would do him good, not harm (12).

• He also noticed her accomplishments and praised her for them (29).

• He saw her good efforts and, rather than being intimidated by this strong woman, he encouraged her endeavors (11-12).

- He, along with his children, rose up and called her blessed (28).

- He acknowledged her faith (20).

- He desired that she be rewarded for her hard work (31).

Many men desire a Proverbs 31 wife, but they have not considered their responsibility to be a Proverbs 31 husband. Paul speaks of this reciprocal relationship in Ephesians 5. Wives are to submit to their husbands, but husbands are to love their wives as Christ loved the church. Husbands have a responsibility to lead their wives toward holiness, but wives, don't miss the role you play. As you submit to his godly leadership, you are encouraging him to lead more and love you better. Likewise, husbands, you will discover that the more you lead and love your wife, the more willing she will be to submit to your leadership.

Marriage is a sanctifying endeavor. The one-flesh union of marriage creates a kind of intimacy that makes hiding almost impossible. All your sin, selfishness, and flaws are laid bare in marriage. But godly marriages need not end when sinfulness becomes visible; godly couples recognize that growth is possible and necessary—that even sin can be forgiven and hurt can be overcome.

Growth is necessary because marriage is more than a physical or civic union. According to Paul, marriage is a picture of Christ's relationship to his church. When God gave us marriage, he intended for it to be a defense of the church—a picture for the world to see how Christ loves and cares for his bride. But how do we get there?

In his book, *This Momentary Marriage*, John Piper shows that with a foundation rooted in the person and work of Christ, marriages can display God's love to the world through loving forgiveness and forbearance. As you are reading this, remember that all of God's word was written to you, whether you are married or single. And all of that Word applies to you, whether you are

> All of God's word was written to you whether you are married or single.

married or single. Therefore, our instruction for marriage is not wrapped up solely in the passages of Scripture dealing with marriage. Any passage of Scripture that gives us guidance for how we should live holy lives, love our neighbors, and interact with others in light of the gospel applies to every aspect of our lives—especially within our marriage relationships.

With this understanding, Piper applies Colossians 3:12-19 to the context of marriage. As God's holy and beloved children, we are to put on "compassionate hearts, kindness, humility, meekness, and patience." Those instructions are not limited to Sunday morning gatherings. Christians are to be clothed in Christlikeness at all times, and especially at home. But Paul goes further in Colossians 3:13: "Bearing with one another, and if one has a complaint against another, forgiving each other; as the Lord has forgiven you, so you also must forgive."

Bear with one another. That doesn't sound very romantic. Of course, divorce isn't romantic either. When we take the term literally, it has even more impact. The word bear literally means to endure. Writing to a local church, Paul urges its members to endure one another and to forgive—to "freely give" good for evil. If this is true in a local church, it is certainly true in marriage.

Married couples are two sinners joined together, and sinners will sin. Sinners will mess up. Sinners will let others down, but Christ's love is shown to the world when spouses choose to bear with one another's failures and to forgive those failures. Additionally, with each act of forgiveness and forbearance, we become a little more like Jesus.

> Marriage isn't always candy and flowers. Often the times of struggle bring the greatest progress.

Marriage isn't always candy and flowers. Sometimes it is forbearance and forgiveness. And it is often during times of struggle that the greatest progress is made.

As I mentioned earlier, I enjoy strength training. I like to pick up heavy things and put them down. Many people believe that lifting heavy weights makes a person strong, but that is only partially true. Strength training requires lifting heavy things, *and* adequate rest, *and* adequate nutrition. Lifting weights produces great stress on the body. As weight is lifted, muscle fibers are torn apart and broken down. Muscle growth occurs during the rest and refueling phases that follow a training session. The greatest gains in strength will come on the back end of the most grueling periods of exercise because the human body responds to stress and strain in the muscles by repairing and rebuilding. But without proper rest and nutrition, the necessary repairs and rebuilding are not possible.

Just like strength training, the most sanctifying times in your life and your marriage will often be the most difficult, because stress can produce spiritual growth. However, for spiritual growth to occur, the stress must be handled appropriately. Muscles only grow in response to stress in a healthy body. In an unhealthy body, stress to the system may result in great damage. Likewise, sanctification is more likely to occur in healthy marriages than in unhealthy ones. Healthy marriages are made up of individuals who bear with one another and forgive, because their commitment is rooted in Christ.

Healthy couples who are grounded in Christ and are mutually committed to one another have marriages that endure precisely because they are *not* addicted to feelings and romance. Romance is fleeting and feelings fade, but a Christ-based commitment can stand the test of time. When couples can look beyond the horizon of their present difficulties to the goal of presenting Christ's love to the world, they can bear with one another, and when they bear with one another long enough, they experience sanctifying growth. But how can you get there? How can you become a sanctifying agent in your spouse's life?

Pursue Christ Personally

If you hope to help your spouse look more like Jesus, the first place to start is with you. Spiritual warfare begins with a battle against your own flesh, and the battle for the soul of your spouse begins with your own personal battle against your own sin. If nothing else, by pursuing Christ, you lead by example and you set the tone in your marriage relationship.

But of course, pursuing Jesus does more than simply set the tone. As you fellowship with Christ personally, you grow in holiness. You begin to look and behave more like Jesus. You walk as a child of light, and you can "discern what is pleasing to the Lord."[1] As you spend time with Christ, you are conformed more and more into his image. You begin to look like the person you were created to be. In other words, you become the kind of spouse Jesus would have you to be. Husbands, when your wife is happy to be married to you and finds your relationship to be a source of joy and satisfaction, she

---

[1] Ephesians 5:10

is more likely to pursue the Jesus who brought about that kind of change in your life. She wants what you have. Ladies, the same is true for you as well. Peter tells us as much in 1 Peter 3:1, "Likewise, wives, be subject to your own husbands, so that even if some do not obey the word, they may be won without a word by the conduct of their wives."

> Your actions have a profound effect on the spiritual life of your spouse.

The message of Scripture is that your actions have a profound effect on the spiritual life of your spouse, and nothing will affect your actions as much as your relationship with Christ.

Provide Space and Time for Your Spouse to Pursue Christ Devotionally

My wife is a busy woman. She takes on the primary responsibility for caring for our home and is more involved in raising our children than I am. She is busy when her feet hit the floor every morning and is often still working until she lies down for bed at night. Many times, the best way for me to care for her soul is to provide space and time for her to pursue Christ on her own. Sometimes this is as simple as me making the bed and doing a load of laundry so that she has time to get into the Word. Other times, the kids and I have

> Carve out time so your spouse can pursue Christ without being burdened by the urgent needs of life.

had a daddy night so that she can gather with other women for accountability, prayer, and/or Bible study.

Regardless of how this looks in your own life, the principle remains the same. Part of the battle for the soul of your spouse can be waged by carving out time so that they can pursue Christ without being burdened by the urgent needs of life.

Pursue Christ Together

There are reasons that many Sunday School classes in the past were divided by sex. It was (and among some age groups, it continues to be) common to see the women's class and the men's class meet separately. The husband and wife drove together in the same car to the church building, walked in, and then went their separate ways. The ladies' classes were often named after a saintly woman from years gone by in the church or after Biblical figures like *Dorcas*. The men's classes were usually called something like *Senior Adult Men 1* because, apparently, we men lack the imagination to create good names for our classes.

I contend that meeting separately from your spouse is not the best way to meet in small groups, but regardless of whether you meet separately or together, it is imperative that you find ways to pursue Christ as a couple. You can pursue Christ publicly by worshiping together and privately through Bible reading, prayer, and even fasting. Listen to sermons together in the car or sing worship songs together in the kitchen. One of the ways Angela and I have pursued Christ together in the past is through a marriage seminar or retreat. We have benefited as participants and as leaders. Interestingly, when we lead seminars or retreats, we usually grow closer in our relationship, just as those who attend the seminar grow closer in relationships.

Regularly Communicate Commitment

Within a marriage, the process of growing in holiness often requires each spouse to say difficult things to the other and to apologize when they have done wrong. Those hard conversations are only possible within the safety of a committed marriage.

For real growth to take place, both spouses need to know that there is no danger of the marriage dissolving because of a disagreement or a tiff. One way to create a feeling of safety within the marriage covenant is to regularly communicate commitment to one another. If the only time you tell your wife you are committed to her is after a fight, you're not communicating commitment well. Make opportunities to remind one another that you are each committed to your marriage. You can do this with cute notes or unexpected flowers. You can also communicate commitment face-to-face while you wait for the rice to boil.

Picture the scene. Kids are screaming. The dog just tracked muddy paw prints through the house. There is a Lego minefield in the den. A Barbie with a missing leg is lying on the kitchen table. And you walk in. You've had a long day and just want to eat and veg out with the newspaper (I know, I'm basically a 70-year-old man in a 40-something body). Instead, you walk into a war zone, and your wife resembles a POW. She is standing at the stove top wild-eyed and exhausted waiting for the rice to boil so that you can attempt to sit everyone down at the table and have a *ahem* *family dinner*. You take her by the hand and say something like this. "I'm so thankful that I'm married to you—I wouldn't want to do life with anyone else."

You just lifted your wife and washed her weary soul. That simple act strengthens your marriage. By regularly cultivating your commitment to one another, you earn the opportunity to not merely survive the hard times, but to mature spiritually through them.

Carry the Load

If you are the kind of person who would drop

everything to help a friend in need, make sure you are the kind of spouse who would do the same thing when your husband or wife is in need. Do you want

> Do you want to grow in holiness as a couple? Bear one another's burdens.

to grow in holiness as a couple? Bear one another's burdens. Pray for your spouse. Pray with your spouse. Pray over your spouse. Go behind their backs and get them the help they need if necessary. You will be amazed to discover how much God works to sanctify you and your spouse as you seek to carry each other. Jesus came not to be served, but to serve. Similarly, we enter our marriages to serve one another. As we seek to live more Christ-like toward our spouses, God works to mold and shape us into his image.

Some people might say that I have a bad wife, because my wife does some things that many wives do not do. Sometimes she tears me down. She has been known to talk about me behind my back. She speaks when I do not want her to speak. On the surface, all of this seems detrimental to our marriage. However, the surface is not the whole story.

This can be illustrated with a story from the end of August 2010. On that Sunday, we held our last service in our old sanctuary. That Sunday was incredible. We baptized a bunch of folks, the building was packed to overflowing, I preached with great freedom, and the Spirit of God moved. People joined our church. People confessed sin and rededicated their lives to Jesus. I should have been the most excited human being on the planet, but instead, I was a ball of negative emotions. Out of nowhere, I found myself under intense spiritual attack and teetering on the edge of an odd despair. The black dog of depression was growling at my door.

After the service, I greeted people at the main door of the sanctuary, as is my habit, and then went to my office to cry. Angela found me. To say I was embarrassed is an understatement, but there I was, a bundle of emotions crumpled in my desk chair, and there, my wife worked to join me under my spiritual load and bear the burden with me. She sat with me and prayed for me and prayed over me. She literally laid her hands and face on me and prayed. I have no idea what she prayed, but I knew then and I know now that I was not all alone. It is great not to be alone, because God said it is not good for man to be alone. He created a suitable helpmate for me, and one of her jobs as my wife, and one of my jobs as her husband, is to bear the burdens of life together.

I have a wife who tears me down, and that is a good thing. You see, like clay in the potter's hands, I am only usable before my Heavenly Father when I'm pliable. Often, I need to be reminded who I am and whose I am. As we drove home from church on another Sunday morning, I griped. I griped about my sermon, and I griped about the church's unwillingness to respond to my message. And then it happened. I asked her what she thought about the sermon, and she destroyed it—and me. "What are you doing?" she asked. "You are a preacher. You are called to preach God's word. You're not a comedian, and you are not an entertainer. I don't know what you did today, but you did not preach."

I was angry and hurt. Then, I was remorseful and repentant. Then, I was thankful. I was thankful (and continue to be so) that God has given me a wife who is willing to speak his words and his calling into my life when I lose my own way. What a blessing to have a wife who is willing to tear me down and then build me up. The conversation didn't end with "you did not preach." Angela went on to remind me that God had called me to preach and that I was able to preach, and she urged me to live out my calling. What a woman.

My wife talks about me behind my back. Behind my back, she praises me, and that is awesome. Behind my back, she will also pray for me and request prayers for me, which is fantastic. Behind my back, she is also willing to reach out to our friends and my accountability partners to get me the help I need when I need it. I'm so glad she is willing to talk about me behind my back, because sometimes my pride prevents her from discussing my needs with others in my presence. Angela is the wife I want and the wife I need. I love her deeply, and she loves me.

My wife is willing to confront me. Not too long ago,

Angela took me by my hands and lovingly rebuked me. She showed me how I had been short with her and with others in my life. She told me she loved me and that she knew I was tired, and then she dropped the hammer, "but you have been short with me, with the kids, and you were rude to others at church tonight. You need to apologize. There is no excuse for you treating others this way."

Was I angry in that moment that my wife was not submitting to me? Did she sin? If you are asking those questions, then you have a perverted understanding of marriage and Paul's commands in Ephesians chapter 5.

The truth is that I don't have a good wife, I have a great, godly wife. I have a wife who is willing to speak when I don't want to hear her talk. She's willing to speak words of encouragement and grace into my life when I'm discouraged and want to wallow in self-pity. She speaks to me about the need for God's grace in my own life, and the victory of God's grace in the lives of others, even when I do not see it (or do not want to see it). She hears me whining and reminds me out loud of Philippians 2:14, "Do all things without grumbling or disputing."

> The church should be filled with couples who oppose their spouse, tear them down, and talk behind their backs for God's glory and their good.

Angela is my wife. She is always fighting for me, even when it means opposing me to my face, tearing me down, and talking behind my back. May the church be filled with couples who oppose their spouse, tear them down, and talk behind their backs for God's glory and their good.

This is what it looks like to carry the load for each other. Carrying the load is not always easy, and it is not always pretty. Carrying the load will occasionally mean doing what you do not want to do—and maybe even doing things that your spouse doesn't want from you in that moment either. But when you become aware that your spouse is struggling under the load of life, you have the privilege and responsibility of bearing that burden. As you bear one another's burdens, you fight for your spouse, and you strengthen your bond.

Set Boundaries

If you do all of the things listed above and spend much time in spiritual disciplines, and yet neglect to protect yourself from the sin that enters your home through media and entertainment choices, you are likely to lose the spiritual battle for your family. Much of what constitutes entertainment today is not conducive to Christian growth. All Christians have a responsibility to set boundaries for the way they will consume media, and married couples are no exception. But for couples with children, this responsibility is doubled. You have the responsibility to guard your own heart and mind and to guard the heart and mind of your children. The battle for holiness in your home must certainly involve Netflix, YouTube, and iTunes, as well as all the other media outlets.

You should also establish boundaries for your social media use. Does your spouse know your passwords? Does your wife know that you are friends on Facebook with your ex-girlfriend? Does your husband know that you regularly interact on Snapchat with men from work? The kinds of boundaries you set on social media may differ from the ones Angela and I have established for our family, but boundaries must exist and be mutually agreed upon. In certain situations, the best approach to social media may be to avoid it altogether.

Fighting for holiness in your life and in the life of your spouse will require regular conversations about what is necessary and appropriate in your marriage. Husbands, as the leaders in your home, you should take the initiative in setting boundaries. Carve out time to think carefully with your wife about when, where, and how you should consume media as individuals, as a couple, and as a family. And then, together, stick to your guns. The battle for holiness is just that, a battle. It is not easy, but it is worthwhile. Pursue Christ, pursue one another, and set boundaries to protect your marriage from the invasion of the world.

Holiness doesn't happen on its own. You will not naturally drift toward holiness. The spiritual struggle against the flesh and the world is real. Our flesh longs to be selfish and self-serving. The world urges us to get our needs met within a marriage or to get out. And yet, the biblical picture is one of self-sacrifice and love. You will not grow in holiness individually or as a couple without a fight, but the fight is worth the effort. For those who overcome, there is laid up a crown of righteousness. Fight to win the crown that never perishes.

> Holiness doesn't happen on its own. You will not naturally drift toward holiness.

PRACTICAL APPLICATION

The Armor of God

10 Finally, be strong in the Lord and in the strength of his might. 11 Put on the whole armor of God, that you may be able to stand against the schemes of the devil. 12 For we do not wrestle against flesh and blood, but against the rulers, against the authorities, against the cosmic powers over this present darkness, against the spiritual forces of evil in the heavenly places. 13 Therefore take up the whole armor of God, that you may be able to withstand in the evil day, and having done all, to stand firm. 14 Stand therefore, having fastened on the belt of truth, and having put on the breastplate of righteousness, 15 and, as shoes for your feet, having put on the readiness given by the gospel of peace. 16 In all circumstances take up the shield of faith, with which you can extinguish all the flaming darts of the evil one; 17 and take the helmet of salvation, and the sword of the Spirit, which is the word of God, 18 praying at all times in the Spirit, with all prayer and supplication. To that end, keep alert with all perseverance, making supplication for all the saints, 19 and also for me, that words may be given to me in opening my mouth boldly to proclaim the mystery of the gospel, 20 for which I am an ambassador in chains, that I may declare it boldly, as I ought to speak.

Ephesians 6:10-20

Spiritual warfare is real, but God has not left his people defenseless. Ephesians 6:10-20 is the passage of Scripture most referred to about spiritual warfare. There, Paul gives insight for believers as they seek to live lives committed to Christ.

> Spiritual warfare is real, but God has not left his people defenseless.

There are six pieces to the armor of God, as Paul describes it, and there are particular ways that each piece of this armor should be used to enable believers to stand against the schemes of the devil.

1. The belt of truth (6:14)— The devil is the father

of lies, and he lies to distort the truth and lead believers astray. God has given you the belt of truth to combat Satan's lies and practice discernment. By immersing yourself in the Bible regularly, you grow in your understanding of who God is and what he desires, and you will be better able to differentiate between God's truths and Satan's lies.

2. **Breastplate of righteousness (6:14)**— The breastplate of righteousness is not primarily about your own good deeds, but rather about the imputed righteousness of Christ.[1] You can overcome Satan's schemes because Jesus has taken your sin and given you his righteousness, making you fit to be accepted into God's presence.

3. **Feet fitted with the gospel of peace (6:15)**— You've been made right with God through the shed blood of Jesus, and you have been given the mission of being a gospel peacemaker throughout the world. The gospel is not just for you; you are called to be ready always to share the good news of Christ's gospel with the world around you.

4. **The shield of faith (6:16)**— Satan will attack your faith, but his fiery darts can be extinguished when you hide behind your faith in God. God

---
[1] Romans 4:22-25

will keep his promises, and as a result, the attacks of Satan cannot prevail. Keep your faith firmly rooted in God's goodness toward you, even when Satan tempts you to doubt.

5. **The Helmet of Salvation (6:17)**— You have confessed your sin and called upon the name of the Lord for salvation. You are secure in the hand of Christ, and no one can snatch you out.[2] Satan can accuse, and he can lie, but he can never undo what God has done in your salvation. Walk in confidence knowing that you belong to Christ.

> Walk in confidence knowing that you belong to Christ.

6. **The Sword of the Spirit, which is the Word of God (6:17)**— The word of God is the only offensive weapon given to believers. When Jesus was confronted by Satan in the wilderness, Jesus opposed him by quoting the Bible to him. God's word is living and active and sharper than any two-edged sword[3], and it is the great hope of the believer in times of trouble.

Finally, Paul urges believers to always pray. God is ready to hear and respond to his children in days of trouble. And remember, the goal is to stand. There may

> The goal is to stand. You may feel like you do not make any progress. Do not worry and do not fret. Cling to the armor of God.

---
[2] John 10:28
[3] Hebrews 4:12

> Hold your ground with confidence that God holds you fast.

be days or months of struggle in your life when you feel like you do not make any progress because of the opposition of the Evil One. In those days, do not worry and do not fret. Cling to the Armor of God and hold your ground with confidence that God holds you fast. You may not make progress, but do not give ground. You are Christ's, and he is yours, and you are safe and secure with him.

CHAPTER SEVEN

Physical Health

Beloved, I pray that all may go well with you and that you may be in good health, as it goes well with your soul.

3 John 1:2

3 John is a unique book in the New Testament. It is a warm and personal letter written by the aged apostle, John, to a man named Gaius to warn him about a false teacher and to urge him to continue to serve the Lord

faithfully. However, John is not all business. He takes time to offer words of care and concern. He refers to Gaius as his "dear friend" and tells him he prays for his prosperity and good health.

John wants more from Gaius than for him to simply succeed in his ministry. John wants Gaius to be filled with the Spirit of God and to enjoy prosperity and good health. John is concerned for Gaius, as his friend and colleague, and he also celebrates that Gaius remains faithful to the truth.

As believers, we should be maturing in wisdom through daily reading of God's word and through prayer; growing in favor with God and with people through sharing the Good News, intentional hospitality, and service; and we should be maturing in stature by living a life that is worthy of the respect of others and by adopting a healthy lifestyle. Just as John desired good health for Gaius, so, too, should we desire good health for ourselves and for our brothers and sisters in Christ.

Glorify God with Your Body

God desires for you to be in good health so that you can glorify him with your body. God is concerned about your health. Many of the Old Testament laws were designed to keep people free from sickness and disease, and Jesus demonstrated His concern for physical health in the New Testament by healing many people.

Certainly, your physical health is secondary to your spiritual health, but it still matters. Your physical health either helps or hinders your spiritual health in the battle for your family. Do you have the lung capacity to go for a walk with your wife? Are you able to get up and down off the floor to play with your kids? Can you throw a ball with your boys or set a volleyball for your girls?

> Your physical health either helps or hinders your spiritual health in the battle for your family.

It is necessary that you learn self-discipline as far as what you take into your body and what you do with it because the body God gave you is a tool for his glory, your good, and the good of the world around you. You must strive to avoid practices that you know are harmful to your body and embrace practices that you know are beneficial. Doing so allows you to be more present for your family and to fight for their success.

From Creation onward, God's desire has been for His people to be both spiritually and physically healthy.

Physical Health Affects Spiritual Health

How does your physical health affect your spiritual health? Just as John wanted Gaius to be physically and spiritually healthy, God desires you to be spiritually and physically healthy as well. Your body is a gift from

God, and you should practice good stewardship in caring for it.

> *Do you not know that you are God's temple and that God's Spirit dwells in you? If anyone destroys God's temple, God will destroy him. For God's temple is holy, and you are that temple.[1]*

A teenager with her first car is a sight to behold. She beams with pride over her new ride. The tires shine and the paint gleams. In the first few weeks with a new car, it can seem at times like that young woman is going to wash the paint right off the car because she cleans it so often.

Your body is a gift from God that deserves far more care than a young person gives to her first car. Paul reminds the Corinthians that they are God's temple and warns them to take care of God's temple. When you read that your body is a temple of God, you are reminded to remember the Old Testament temple. The temple was not just a place of gathering; it represented the actual presence of God among the children of Israel. God's Spirit lived in the temple.

> Your body is a gift from God, and you should practice good stewardship in caring for it.

---

[1] 1 Corinthians 3:16-17

Living Sanctuary

When you think of your body as the temple of God, does it affect the places where you go or the activities you engage in? Our bodies are a living sanctuary.

> *Or do you not know that your body is a temple of the Holy Spirit within you, whom you have from God? You are not your own, for you were bought with a price. So glorify God in your body.*[2]

Paul says our bodies are a temple of the Holy Spirit, but how did that happen? If the temple in the Old Testament was a building in Jerusalem, how is it possible that Paul could now say that the bodies of believers are a temple of the Holy Spirit? When Jesus died on the cross, something magnificent happened.

In Matthew's account, he wrote:

> *And behold, the curtain of the temple was torn in two, from top to bottom. And the earth shook, and the rocks were split.*[3]

The curtain that Matthew mentions separated the most holy place in the temple from the rest of the temple. The most holy place was where the Ark of the Covenant was kept and where the Spirit of God resided. Only the high priest was allowed to enter that area

---

[2] 1 Corinthians 6:19-20
[3] Matthew 27:51

of the temple, and even he was only allowed to enter once each year on the Day of Atonement. When Jesus died on the cross, the curtain in the temple was torn. The sacrifice for sin was complete, and all believers were given access to the Spirit of God. Access to God's presence was gained by the greatest sacrifice the world has ever known. Jesus gave his life so that Christians could have the Holy Spirit take up permanent residence in their lives.

The Holy Spirit was given to believers as a gift of God's presence after Jesus rose from the grave and ascended to heaven.[4] If you are a Christian reading this book, the Holy Spirit of God lives within you. Because you have the Holy Spirit, you are enabled to serve the Lord and fulfill his purposes. As a Christian, your body has become the temple of God—the dwelling place of God—and you have a responsibility to care well for it.

> Caring well for God's temple includes taking intentional steps to make sure that your body functions in the way that God designed it to function.

Caring well for your body (the temple of God) certainly includes practicing spiritual disciplines—corporate worship, regular Bible reading, prayer, evangelism, etc.—but that is not all. Caring well for God's temple also includes taking intentional steps to ensure that your body

---

[4] Acts, Chapter 2

functions in the way that God designed it to function. It also means taking care of your body so that you are best able to do the things God has called you to do. It is difficult for you to discharge your responsibilities as a parent, a teacher, a pastor, a firefighter, or a whole list of other things if you are obese, drunk, or just always tired because of your poor lifestyle choices.

Self-Control and Self-Discipline

Potty training is rarely an enjoyable experience for parents. It is difficult to understand why kids don't want to use the toilet and how in the world they can be comfortable wearing wet clothes. Often, what is even worse than the frustration of the actual potty training is the techniques used to try to convince kids to use the facilities. There are rewards and punishments. There are warnings and praises. Then, worst of all, there is Elmo.

Elmo's Potty Time is a video created to try to help kids learn to use the bathroom (or so they claim; it may have been created to mock parents by making potty training look so simple that a whiny puppet can do it, who knows). For most adults, Elmo is annoying. However, even more annoying is seeing your kid watch Elmo for the 50th time as he excitedly reminds her to use the potty, only to see her wet herself in the middle of the den floor.

It just isn't fair.

But kids have to be taught to use the potty because self-control and discipline are not innate characteristics; they are learned traits. Even as adults, self-control and discipline can be difficult. If you are going to live a healthy lifestyle, it won't happen by accident. You have to commit to doing the hard things—spending time with the Lord, getting adequate sleep, eating right, maintaining a healthy level of activity, and spending ample time outside, just to name a few.

The Apostle Paul knew the value of discipline. He longed to share the gospel and to live a life honoring the Lord. As a result of his desire to honor Christ, he disciplined his body and brought it under strict control so that he could preach well and not be disqualified.

> Physical self-control and discipline help you to grow spiritually.

Taking care of your physical health impacts every area of your life. When writing to the church at Corinth, Paul needed to correct some false teaching about the proper foods that Christians could eat. There was controversy over whether or not food that had been killed in sacrifice to idols should be eaten.

> *"All things are lawful," but not all things are helpful. "All things are lawful," but not all things build up. Let no one seek his own good, but the good of his neighbor. Eat whatever is sold in the meat market without raising any question on the ground of conscience. For "the earth is the Lord's,*

> *and the fullness thereof." If one of the unbelievers invites you to dinner and you are disposed to go, eat whatever is set before you without raising any question on the ground of conscience. But if someone says to you, "This has been offered in sacrifice," then do not eat it, for the sake of the one who informed you, and for the sake of conscience—I do not mean your conscience, but his. For why should my liberty be determined by someone else's conscience?[5]*

Paul's answer to the Corinthians was that they should be more concerned with how their actions affected others than with anything else. Christians are free to eat and drink whatever pleases them, so long as they don't cause others to stumble. And then, Paul offers one other caveat: "Whatever you do, do everything for the glory of God."

The great Southern storyteller and comedian, Jerry Clower, was once asked by a group of students, "What is right and wrong?" His answer was a short question: "Can you thank the Good Lord for the opportunity he has given you to do this thing you are considering?" In his own way, Jerry Clower restated the words of Paul.

When we consider what we eat and drink, we need to ask, "Does this food or drink bring glory to God?" Your body is a gift that deserves your attention. How is

---

[5] 1 Corinthians 10:23-29

the food or

drink that you are putting into your body bringing glory to God? Are your exercise habits bringing glory to God?

Increased Capacity to Serve God

It is impossible for you to control every aspect of your health. You can't determine your genes, you may have little control over the amount of pollution you are exposed to, and you have no control over the home where you grew up. But you can control much of your health. You can determine what you eat and drink, your level of physical activity, and you can decide whether you will smoke, consume alcohol, or keep your coffee intake at a reasonable level.

> Physical health increases your capacity to serve others and serve the Lord.

It is true that some things lie outside of your control, but you must not worry about the things that you cannot control. Instead, you can work to be a faithful steward of the body God has given you. You can make efforts to practice good health, and in so doing, you can increase your capacity to serve God. John Piper explains how bodily training increases capacity to serve the Lord this way,

> *My main motive for exercise is purity and productivity. By purity, I mean being a more loving person (as Jesus said, "love your neighbor," Mat-*

thew 22:39). By productivity, I mean getting a lot done (as Paul said, "abounding in the work of the Lord," 1 Corinthians 15:58).... In short, I have one life to live for Jesus (2 Corinthians 5:15). I don't want to waste it. My approach is not mainly to lengthen it, but to maximize purity and productivity now.'[6]

Increased Capacity to Fight for Your Family

As you fight for your family, your physical health plays an important role in your ability to thrive. When you prioritize your health, you are more able to love your spouse well. Husbands who are physically fit are more able to lead in their home, play with their kids, and protect their family if and when the need arises—you have the mental and spiritual energy to do what it takes to love your wife well. Wives who work to advance their physical fitness often find it easier to love their husbands and be loved; they also have the necessary energy and physical ability to play with their kids and to interact well with the world around them. But that isn't all. Physical health increases your capacity to serve others and serve the Lord.

You could argue that exercise is essential to make

---

[6] Piper, John. "Brothers, Bodily Training Is of Some Value," in *Brothers, We are Not Professionals*, exp. ed. (B&H, 2013), p. 186-187.

you a better parent as well. Exercise is important for parents because it alleviates anxiety and depression and releases "feel-good" hormones[7]. By managing stress in your life, you enhance your parenting opportunities. Exercise is also a wonderful way to spend family time. You can set family exercise goals and make it fun. Remember, you can take family walks, play kickball, or go for a group swim. Some research even suggests that families who exercise together have stronger family bonds and kids with increased motivation and accountability[8].

Moms and dads who are physically fit set the standard for health for which their kids can strive. Healthy parents also set their children up to live healthier lives. Perhaps even more important, parents who are healthy can play with their kids and care for their physical needs more easily. Parents who prioritize their health are usually sick less often and spend less time out of the fight. Long-term, parents who prioritize their health in their 30s and 40s can maintain their health long enough to enjoy their grandchildren and to invest in their adult children.

Couples who prioritize physical health also have more opportunities to cultivate commitment. Whether it is long walks together, marathon training, rucks, or

---

[7] uknow.uky.edu/uk-healthcare/exercising-and-self-care-important-parents

[8] santovia.com/blog/the-benefits-of-family-exercise-on-health-and-happiness/

weight training sessions, physical fitness can be a terrain couples explore together. Through times of mutual exercise, you will find lots of opportunities to affirm one another and to build one another up in accordance with Paul's words in 1 Thessalonians 5:11, "Therefore encourage one another and build one another up..."

Physically fit people have improved self-confidence, increased energy levels, and better long-term health outcomes. Further, fit couples report higher libido than people who do not prioritize their physical fitness, and thus make the 1 Corinthians 7 command to meet one another's sexual needs more enjoyable.

How Do You Get There?

For many of you reading this, you don't have to be convinced that physical fitness is important. Instead, you are trying to figure out how in the world you can do all of the things that this book tells you to do. How are you going to fit one more thing into your life?

Maybe you've seen someone illustrate time management with a jar and rocks. If you put the big rocks into the jar first, you're able to get all the rocks and sand into the jar. But if you start with the small stuff, you don't have any room for the big rocks.

To help me keep the big rocks in the right place, I use a series of habits called 7-STRONG every day (you can learn more about 7-STRONG at www.7-strong.org). The habits are:

1. Read God's word.
2. Spend five minutes in silent prayer.
3. Be around people who want what's best for you.
4. Eat healthy foods.
5. Sleep seven to eight hours every night.
6. Exercise for at least thirty minutes.
7. Get outside for at least thirty minutes.

Begin by arranging the big rocks first. You don't have time to eat healthy and exercise because there are too many other things competing for your time. If you believe that your health is important, consider rearranging things in your life to prioritize it. Cut out a TV show, stop doom-scrolling on your phone, or go to bed 30 minutes earlier to allow yourself time to walk in the morning.

Here are more ways you might create time to exercise:

- Go for a walk while your kid is at dance practice instead of waiting in the car.
- Join a gym near your work so you can exercise during your lunch break.
- Celebrate small windows for activity. Not every workout has to last an hour; if you have 20 minutes, go for a short run or do jumping jacks or air squats.

- Find an activity that you enjoy. The best exercise for you is the one you will do.
- Stop buying junk food (then you can't be tempted to eat it at midnight).
- Eat your vegetables. Seriously. It makes a difference.
- Consider restricting your daily eating time to an eight-hour window, which can help reduce your caloric intake.
- Go for a walk when you make phone calls.
- Put exercise on your schedule and stick to it.
- Exercise as a couple. Play tennis. Go for a ruck. Pick up pickleball or go for a hike.

Finally, prioritize exercise that gives you the most bang for your buck. Avoid fad exercise routines that do not improve your overall physical fitness or that take an inordinate amount of your time. If you struggle to make time to exercise, then by all means, maximize the limited time you have available. For instance, the average man can burn about 160 calories (one serving of Oreos) on a 30-minute walk. But if that man carries a 30-pound backpack and increases his speed a little, he can burn 2 times or even 3 times as many calories. If you have a limited amount of time to exercise, make the most of every minute. Few exercises are as efficient for overall health as rucking (which is just walking with weight in a backpack). You can start rucking by putting a few books or bags of sand in a backpack and going for a walk. If you want to increase the weight without spending a lot of money, you can buy a forty-pound bag of playground sand at your local home improvement store for less than $10.

Other forms of efficient exercise include high-intensity interval training (HIIT), rowing, and large-muscle weight-lifting exercises.

Lifting weights burns calories and changes body composition. Strength training also adds muscle mass and can increase bone density. Lifting weights is literally an insurance policy for your body as you age. Weight lifting does not have to be incredibly time-consuming, and with a little coaching from a friend or a personal trainer at your local gym, you can become proficient with compound exercises involving kettlebells, dumbbells, and even barbells. Building muscle allows you to burn calories even at rest, thus optimizing the time you spend exercising.

Regardless of what steps you take to improve your overall physical fitness, just know that your physical health is a spiritual issue as well as a physical issue. God is concerned with how you treat the body he has given you, and so is your family. Getting a little healthier and a little stronger today is an important—if often overlooked—step in the process of fighting for your family.

PRACTICAL APPLICATION

When You Have Health Issues Beyond Your Control

But what if you have health issues that are beyond your control? Is there still a place for you in God's service?

YES!

Joni Eareckson Tada is a great example of how God can work powerfully through a person with a disability. After becoming a quadriplegic in a diving accident at age 17, Joni Eareckson Tada continued to serve the Lord and was eventually given a national platform to share the gospel and to advocate for disability ministry. Joni has not allowed her disability to stop her from serving the Lord, and the Lord has certainly not cast her aside because of her disability.

Another great example of a faithful Christian with a disability is Daniel Ritchie. Daniel is an evangelist from Raleigh, North Carolina. Born without arms, Daniel was told by many that he was hopeless, but he learned that God had special plans for him. Daniel is married with children and was elected first vice president of the Southern Baptist Convention in 2025.

> All Christians have a responsibility to care for their bodies as a temple of the Lord.

All Christians have a responsibility to care for their bodies as a temple of the Lord. But if your temple appears to be damaged, just know that you are God's temple nonetheless. Further, know that God does not make mistakes, and you are not a mistake. According to Psalm 139, you are "fearfully and wonderfully made." God still loves you, and God can use you.

No one is perfect. Everyone has something to overcome, but God is enough. Your physical limitations may be more obvious to others, but God is just as able to use you as he is anyone else. Your body is a temple to the Lord, regardless of how it may look to you, and if you will be faithful with the temple God has given you, he can use you for his glory and your good.

Never allow the limitations of your body to be limitations for what God can do in and through you.

CONCLUSION

THE BATTLE OF OUR LIVES

Spiritual Warfare Is Real

If you are going to be victorious, you must acknowledge the real presence of evil forces that want to do you and your family harm. The Bible warns us,

> *We do not wrestle against flesh and blood,*
> *but against the rulers, against the authorities,*

against the cosmic powers over this present darkness, against the spiritual forces of evil in the heavenly places.[1]

Satan is a roaring lion roaming the earth to seek those whom he may devour. Unless you are willing to acknowledge the presence of malevolent forces, you are easy prey.[2]

> Satan is a roaring lion... unless you are willing to acknowledge the presence of malevolent forces, you are easy prey.

Married couples must acknowledge the real challenges that exist so they can remain committed to one another. Parents must recognize that their children are growing up in a post-Christian culture that is antithetical to the gospel and the things of the Lord. Once you have come to grips with the reality that the flesh, the world, and the spiritual realm wage war against your holiness and against your family, you can become equipped to engage the battle.

Marriage Is Hard

Angela ran a half-marathon a few years ago. She set a goal, trained hard, and finished the race. When it was over, she didn't say, "Wow, that was easy," but she did feel the sense of accomplishment that came with

---

[1] Ephesians 6:12
[2] 1 Peter 5:8

a job well done. Almost anything worth doing is hard work. Having a healthy marriage may be the hardest work you will ever do.

One of the greatest lies that must be overcome in marriage is the lie that it is supposed to be easy. When I lead marriage classes, seminars, and retreats, it is always fun to have senior adult couples who have been married for forty years or more. I usually ask them the same question, "Has it always been fun and easy?" They laugh.

Because sin is a reality, husbands and wives don't always have each other's best interests at heart. Rather than leading sacrificially, husbands can be selfish and domineering. Instead of serving gladly, wives can be petty and overbearing. To find success in your marriage, you must come to grips with the fact that marriage is hard. If you got married expecting everything to be peaches and cream, you are likely to find yourself disillusioned.

If Satan can convince you that marriage is supposed to be easy, he can quickly lead you into disappointment when your marriage becomes difficult. Satan's lie festers into even more lies as you feel alienated, believing that your marriage is somehow inferior to all other marriages. You can rescue your marriage from fantasy and bring it into real life. Remember that a good marriage is hard work, and you can do the hard work to have a healthy marriage.

Commitment Is Sexy

Spiritual warfare is more than a battle with Satan and demons. We must also battle against the temptations of the world around us. From advertisers to baristas to your friends at work, the world around you is often at war against committed marriages. When romance seeps out of marriage, the relationship may not feel alluring. However, when marriages are built on a foundation stronger than romance, real intimacy and romance are possible. Commitment through mundane or difficult years of marriage may not sound exciting, but nothing is sexier than a marriage that lasts a lifetime.

You can win the battle for your marriage if you turn conventional wisdom on its head. Commitment through thick and thin, sickness and health, is exhilarating for the long haul. Short skirts and high heels are one kind of sexy, but they're not the best kind. Loving your spouse enough to hold her hair in the middle of a stomach virus or clean a kid's urine-covered bed one more time adds spice to your marriage that gray hair and arthritis can't take away. Commitment creates intimacy and security, and nothing is sexier than that.

Raising Kids Is a Battle All Its Own

Baby pictures are not real life. Smiling, dry, clean babies are a treasure as rare as pure gold. Babies are only cute sometimes, and teenagers are only fun part of the time. Raising kids is a battle against the demonic forces, against the world around you, and even against your own flesh. The whole world seems intent on drawing your kid away from Christ and away from you. Then (especially in moments of sleep deprivation and frustration), your own flesh can seem to rise up in such a way as to drive a wedge between you and your kids. Raising children to know the Lord and pursue holiness requires the real intervention of the Holy Spirit.

> You are not your kids' last great hope. They need Jesus.

You are not your kids' last great hope. They need Jesus. Your role as a parent is to lead them to Christ and lead them into patterns of holiness and righteousness. Introduce them to the church and keep them grounded in the church. Live with them among the people of God and the things of God. The Word of God is your offensive attack for your kids. The defensive attack is against all of the negative things that will assail and assault them.

You are not going to be their best friend. That is OK. You have a much more important role. You are fighting for them, even when they don't understand it or can't see it. Go to war, parents. Don't surrender. Don't give ground. Battle for your kids in prayer and in action, and trust the Lord to go ahead of you.

Sex Is Spiritual Warfare

Read 1 Corinthians 7 and commit it to memory. One of your greatest weapons in spiritual warfare as a married couple is a healthy sex life. What does that look like in your own relationship? You and your spouse have to figure out the specifics, but you can't throw in the towel. Intimacy is not a given for busy couples, but it is a necessity. Husbands, remember that your wife may be more excited if you take out the trash than if you light candles, so do whatever it takes. Ladies, remember, his desire and drive for intimacy may be double what yours is, but that doesn't make him weird—he's just a man.

Safeguard your marriage by making intimacy a regular part of your relationship, and put it on the calendar if you must. Scheduling your intimate encounters may not sound very spicy, but it is far more satisfying than not sex. Do whatever it takes. The devil will create all manner of pseudo-emergencies and distractions to take you away from intimate time with your spouse. You must fight against the temptation to neglect each other and instead invest in intimacy for the health and success of your marriage.

Holiness Is Wholeness

Your marriage is one of your greatest opportunities

to honor Christ with your life. Your marriage is a picture of the relationship between Christ and his church for all the world to see. Your marriage should be characterized by holiness on the part of each partner. Pursue the Lord together through corporate worship and family devotion. Create space for each other to pursue the Lord personally through spiritual disciplines and other discipleship opportunities. Create a culture of holiness in your home and build structures of Bible study and prayer.

A Healthy Lifestyle Is a Spiritual Discipline

The decisions you make for your physical health are spiritual decisions, and they impact more than just you. You should take care of your body because it is the temple of the Holy Spirit. You should also be concerned about your physical health, because it affects your ability to care for your family well. Choosing a healthy lifestyle gives you a better opportunity to fight for your family, and your example encourages your spouse and children to pursue healthy lives as well.

Failure Is Not an Option

Marriage is a battle that you *must* win. What will it cost you to win the spiritual victory for your marriage?

It may cost you nearly everything this world has to offer, but even if it does, it will be worth it. Good marriages honor Christ, and godly marriages bring satisfaction and fulfillment. Hopefully, you've read this book as a safeguard against struggles in your marriage. However, if you have picked this book up because your marriage is on the rocks, keep fighting. Keep your head above water, fight the good fight, finish the race. Marriage is worth the struggle.

> Marriage is a battle you *must* win. It may cost you nearly everything this world has to offer, but even if it does, it will be worth it.

APPENDIX

SPIRITUAL WARFARE AND ORPHAN CARE

Brooklyn and Sloan came to us because Angela and I had submitted to God's prompting in our lives to become foster parents. My plan (note that it was *my* plan) was to foster one child at a time and to one day adopt one of our foster children and become their forever family. God's plan was slightly different. God's plan was for us to bring two children into our home within just a few months of being licensed as foster parents and to finalize their adoption two years later.

Foster care and adoption turned out to be the hardest thing we have ever done in our lives. When two little people who had lived through pain and rejection came into our home, they helped to expose all sorts of ugliness and sin in our lives and welcomed a season of spiritual warfare that we had not known before. We found ourselves struggling against our own attitudes and sinful hearts as well as fighting alongside Sloan and Brooklyn against all of the sin that had been committed against them. It was a family affair, and it was long, and it was often ugly, but there was victory on the other side. Here are ten things about orphan care that will help you find spiritual victory if you step into this world:

1. **It is hard.** It is hard in nearly every conceivable way. It is hard in ways you expect and in ways that you couldn't even imagine. I won't go into details about all of the difficulty, but just know it is hard on everyone (and anyone who says differently on Facebook or Instagram, or wherever else, is not being honest). It is hard on parents and on the kids–the new kids and the existing kids. I would encourage you to pray about fostering and adopting, but I don't want you to walk into it with rose-colored glasses. Meshing two families together is an intense spiritual struggle. Be prepared. Kids aren't goldfish. They take work.

2. **It is lonely.** Many of our family and friends will read this and feel offended by that statement. Please don't. We have been incredibly supported, but it still feels lonely because (as another foster parent so aptly put it), unless you are living it, you really do not understand. Sometimes you feel like you are on an island all by yourself. But there is hope, knowing that as lonely as you feel, you are never all alone or forsaken. [1]

3. **You don't have to do it by yourself.** We have a wonderful family and church family who have cared for us throughout this process. Additionally, we sought out a counselor who helped us navigate the terrain of assimilation. The adoption process can feel very lonely, but you do not need to walk it by yourself. Your church exists, in part, to bear your burdens alongside you.[2] You don't have to do this alone, so don't. Rely on family, church family, and friends. God created us as relational and needy beings. There is no shame in accepting help.

4. **You will get tired of being bragged on.** Imagine this: your kids have been terrible, everyone is miserable, and you've been living a re-

---

[1] Deuteronomy 31:6
[2] Galatians 6:2

peated cycle of losing your cool and apologizing to your kids. In the midst of it, someone looks you in the eye and says, "Wow, you are such a wonderful person. You must feel so blessed." You don't feel wonderful. You feel like a failure. Get ready for it.

5. **There are tons of kids who need to be loved.** At any given time, the state of South Carolina alone will have nearly 4,000 kids in foster care. Orphan care is hard, but there is a need and a biblical expectation for Christians to care for orphans.[3]

6. **Adoption is pro-life, and God is in control.** Before children are formed in the womb, God knows them.[4] God knitted the orphans together in their mother's wombs, too. When we stand against abortion, it is important to recognize that those orphaned children need somewhere to go. Christians have a wonderful opportunity to show orphaned children that just as God loves them, so, too, can they be loved and wanted in this world by God's people.

7. **Adoption is a gospel issue.** If children are not adopted into homes where the gospel is taught, they may never hear the gospel. The

---
[3] James 1:27
[4] Jeremiah 1:5

greatest spiritual warfare we wage is the war for the souls of people. You have an opportunity to see children brought from darkness to light in your own home. You also have an opportunity to be a living illustration of God's love to his children in salvation. We were all once orphans, but God has made us his children through Christ.[5]

8. **The Department of Social Services can be difficult to deal with.** The spiritual battle to care for orphans may not always seem supernatural. At times, the struggle is just dealing with government and non-governmental agencies whose paperwork requirements, interviews, and inspections are incredibly onerous. I won't go into explicit detail; if you have questions, please email me. But don't just send emails, spend time in prayer. Remember, we don't wage war as the world wages war. Pray for God to break down the barriers that keep you from caring for the orphans.[6]

9. **It doesn't have to be expensive.** International adoptions and private adoptions can cost tens of thousands of dollars. We have dear friends who are currently raising money to adopt a child from Haiti. We also have cousins

---
[5] Ephesians 1:5
[6] 2 Corinthians 10:3-5

who adopted from China, and we have other friends who have adopted from Africa and South America. Those routes are right for many people, and I'm thankful for families who have chosen those paths. However, adoption through state agencies doesn't carry the same kind of expense. In many cases, all legal fees are covered by the state. Satan may tell you that you can't afford to foster or adopt, but remember, he is the father of lies.[7]

10. **It is all worth it.** Without a doubt, foster care and adoption are the hardest things Angela and I have ever done, but it is all worth it. On February 10, 2017, we officially became Thompson, party of six, and it was one of the greatest days of our lives. On that day, and on every day since, we have celebrated the gift of all four of our children. Orphan care is hard, and many doubts will come your way, but remember,

> *Children are a heritage from the LORD, offspring a reward from him. Like arrows in the hands of a warrior are children born in one's youth. Blessed is the man whose quiver is full of them. They will not be put to shame when they contend with their opponents in court.*[8]

---
[7] John 8:44
[8] Psalm 127:3-5

Books & Resources

AVAILABLE FROM THE AUTHOR

RESOURCES

VINTAGE CHRISTMAS

The birth of Jesus was prophesied, predicted, foreshadowed, and foretold in the Old Testament. The Old Testament points to Jesus, and Vintage Christmas will help you celebrate Christmas a little differently this year as you understand your Savior more intimately and learn to love the Bible more fully.

Available on Amazon. Purchase links can be found at MakeItOrdinary.org

Through twenty-five devotions, you will grow in your understanding of Jesus through the lens of the Old Testament. Each day's devotion ends with a question to ponder and a short prayer—making it perfect for individual, family, or small group study.

RESOURCES

Home for the Holidays

Home for the Holidays is an Advent devotional that will help you restore hope, love, joy, and peace in your home this Christmas season as you direct your attention to the Savior who was born to rescue the world from the curse of sin.

Available on Amazon. Purchase links can be found at MakeItOrdinary.org

Written for families, the devotions are easy to follow and include scripture, discussion guides, activities, songs, and weekly challenges that you can complete together. You will be encouraged to focus on Christ and to share what you learn with one another and with others outside of your home.

RESOURCES

Next Steps

Becoming part of a church family is a significant decision that should not be taken lightly. As a member of a church, you commit to a spiritual family that provides care, encouragement, accountability, and support for one another, centered around God's word.

> Available on Amazon. Purchase links can
> be found at MakeItOrdinary.org

We want to be open and honest about what we believe and how we work together as a church for the glory of God and the advancement of His kingdom. Individuals and churches can utilize the resources in this book to learn more about belonging to a healthy church family.

RESOURCES

Raised to Life

If you are a new Christian, you are probably asking the question, "Now what?" The Bible gives you the answer for that, and this short guide for new believers will help you as you begin your new journey of faith.

Available on Amazon.

Purchase links can be found at MakeItOrdinary.org

Written for new believers, this guide will answer questions about the Christian faith, baptism, the need for a church family and small group accountability, and guide you in sharing your testimony. Also included is a guide for how to study Scripture.

Podcasts

The Ordinary Christian Podcast is a podcast dedicated to real people like you, seeking to live out your Christian faith in the ordinary aspects of everyday life.

Listen where you stream podcasts or at MakeItOrdinary.org.

The purpose of the 7-STRONG podcast is to share testimonies and tips to equip you with implementing seven habits that make you stronger and more resilient.

Listen where you stream podcasts or at 7-STRONG.org

RESOURCES

Ordinary Virtues & 7-STRONG

The purpose of the virtue initiative is to build character outside of the church through the teaching of traditional virtues and intentional mentoring in schools, teams, secular organizations, businesses, and the corporate world.

For more information, visit MakeItOrdinary.org.

The purpose of the 7-Strong initiative is to equip individuals with seven habits to increase strength and resiliency and make today healthier than yesterday.

For more information, visit 7-STRONG.org.

www.ingramcontent.com/pod-product-compliance
Lightning Source LLC
Chambersburg PA
CBHW020244010526
44107CB00002B/84